W9-CRR-988

American Cornucopia

Distributed by The University Press of Virginia, Charlottesville

American Cornucopia

Treasures of the Winterthur Library

EDITED BY

Katharine Martinez

WINTERTHUR, DELAWARE
THE HENRY FRANCIS DU PONT WINTERTHUR MUSEUM
1990

This project was supported by funds
from the Friends of Winterthur.

LIBRARY OF CONGRESS CATALOGUING-IN-PUBLICATION DATA

Winterthur Library.
    American cornucopia : treasures of the Winterthur Library / edited by
Katharine Martinez.
          p.   cm.
    Includes bibliographical references.
    ISBN 0-912724-20-X
    1. Winterthur Library. 2. Decorative arts—Library resources—Delaware—
Wilmington. 3. Rare books—Library resources—Delaware—Wilmington.
4. United States—Civilization—Library resources—Delaware—Wilmington.
I. Martinez, Katharine, 1950–   . II. Title.
Z733.W785W55   1990
026.973—dc20   90–4115
                                                       CIP

COVER: Printed challis from Swatch Book 65 x 697, France, ca. 1830s–50s.

To
Henry Francis du Pont

Contents

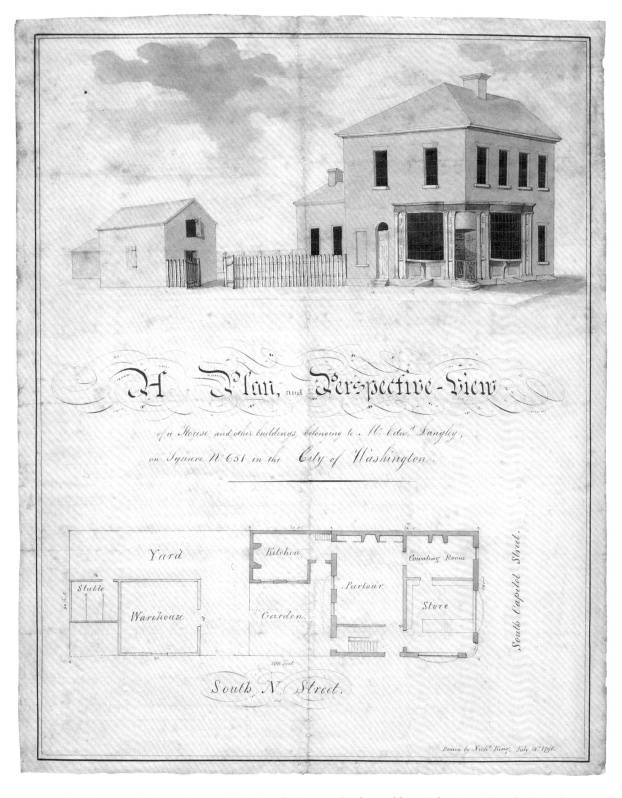

Within the illustration:

A Plan, and Perspective-View

of a House, and other buildings, belonging to Mr. Edwd. Langley,

on Square No. 651 in the City of Washington.

Yard

Kitchen

Counting Room

Stable

Parlour

Warehouse

Garden

Store

100 Feet

South N. Street.

South Capitol Street.

Drawn by Nichs. King. July 14th 1798.

PLATE I. Nicholas King, *A Plan, and Perspective-View of a House and Other Buildings, Belonging to Mr. Edwd. Langley . . .*, 1798. Watercolor; H. 18⅛″, w. 14¾″. ¶ Although the building illustrated here no longer stands, at least one other federal dwelling attributed to Nicholas King is extant in Georgetown, D.C.

76

PLATE 2. Feathers, flower, and leaves. Watercolor; H. 9½″, W. 15″. From Christian M. Nestell, drawing book, New York, 1811/12, p. 76.

PLATE 3. John Lewis Krimmel, woman ironing, July 1819. From Sketchbooks, vol. 5, leaf 8, pl. 18. Watercolor; H. 4⅞″, W. 7″. ¶ A great treasure of the library's, Krimmel's Sketchbooks depict street scenes and domestic interiors, chiefly of Philadelphia. Captivating in their informality, Krimmel's renderings are an important source of information on urban interiors.

PLATE 4. Pompeian wall decoration. From *Magazin für Freunde des guten Geschmacks* 4, no. 5 (1798): pl. 12. Journal: H. 9⅛", W. 10¹⁵⁄₁₆". ¶ As the neoclassical style gained popularity in the late eighteenth and early nineteenth centuries, many luxury magazines appeared, devoting much of their efforts toward the definition and illustration of fashionable taste in dress and decoration. The Leipzig publication from which this illustration is taken depicted interiors done in the Pompeian, Egyptian, and other classically inspired styles. All are exquisitely rendered in color.

PLATE 5. Henry H. Crapo, upstairs bedroom, William J. Rotch house, New Bedford, Mass., ca. 1880. Ink and watercolor; H. 8¼″, w. 13¼″. ¶ This water-color of a room in the Rotch house is one of several executed by Henry H. Crapo (1803–92), who lived in the house between 1872 and 1881. His carefully drawn depictions of the rooms reveal how older furnishings and current fashions were integrated in the late nineteenth century. While the mahogany slant-front desk, the black painted ladder-back chair, and the federal sofa shown in this view are antiques, the Japanese fans, scrolls, and scarves are more recent acquisi-tions. The old leather fire bucket on the floor, perhaps being used as a wastebasket, is inscribed "A. Davis" in recognition of the house's designer.

BEST ENGLISH CHINA.

PLATE 6. "Tea and Breakfast Services / English China Ware." From *Illustrated Pattern Book of English China and Earthenware* . . . (N.p., [ca. 1880]), p. 28. Page: H. 14½″, W. 10¾″. ¶ This array of decorated English porcelain teacups and saucers appears in a glass and ceramic wholesalers' catalogue that offers many types of wares. At least three different wholesalers' names appear in the catalogue, including the unidentified "A.M." of Stoke-on-Trent, Staffordshire, England.

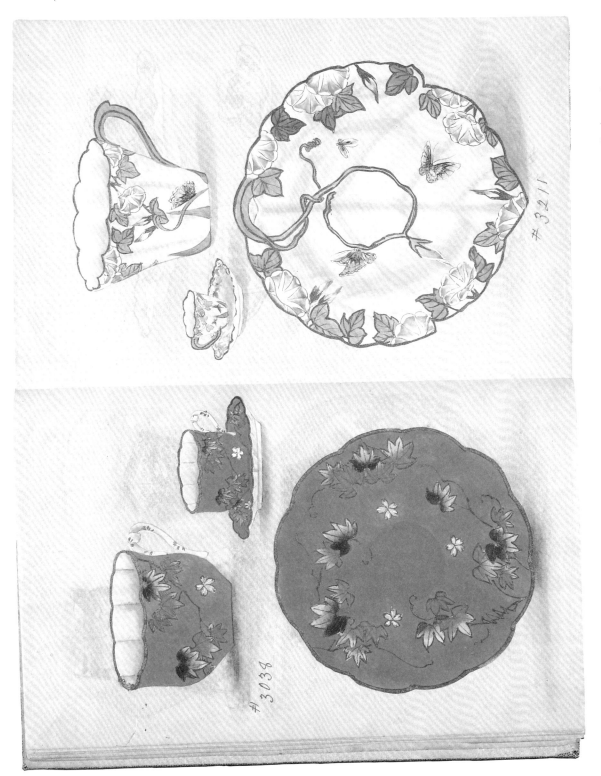

#3211

#3038

PLATE 7. Japanese porcelain. From [*Catalogue Containing Watercolor Drawings of Japanese Porcelain*], vol. 1 (N.p., [n.p., [ca. 1850–99]), pls. 3038, 3211. Watercolor; H. 10½", W. 13¾". ¶ The availability of Japanese goods in the United States accelerated after Matthew Calbraith Perry opened trade with Japan in 1854. These watercolor-ink-and-gold drawings of porcelain cups and saucers were featured along with Japanese earthenwares, porcelains, furniture, and lacquerware. The catalogue's appealing and colorful naturalistic decoration ensured a ready market for Japanese export goods. The wares themselves, however, reflect the taste of Western consumers rather than the Japanese, who preferred more chaste and traditional products.

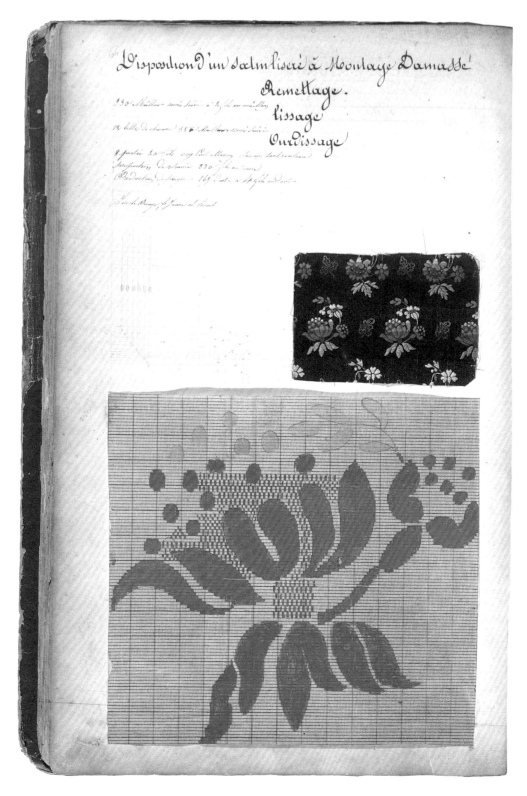

PLATE 8. Leaf from a handloom weaver's draft design book, probably France, nineteenth century. Page: H. 18½″, w. 11½″. ¶ In a happy blend of technology and art, this manuscript combines instructions for weaving floral textiles with full-scale color swatches of fabrics as they were to appear when woven.

PLATE 9. Pavilion bathhouse, upper terrace, Formal Garden, 1915. Autochrome; H. 5″, W. 7″. ¶ Perfected by Lumière Brothers of Lyon, France, in 1907, the autochrome process is generally recognized to be the first form of color photography.

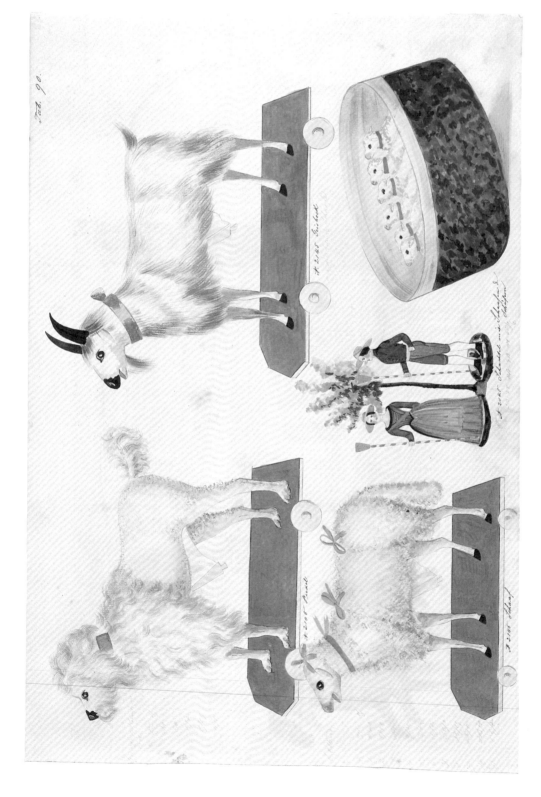

PLATE 10. Poodle, billy goat, sheep, shepherds, and box of sheep. From [*Catalogue of Toys*] (Germany, 1818–39). Watercolor; H. 11½″, W. 18″. ¶ The detailed watercolors of this manuscript catalogue must have made irresistible sales tools. As demonstrated by the items shown here, most of the toys depicted in the catalogue's 135 illustrations are still popular with children today.

Made by C.F.ORVIS, Manchester,Vt.
COPYRIGHTED.

PLATE 11. "Lake Flies." From Mary Orvis Marbury, *Favorite Flies and Their Histories* (Boston and New York: Houghton, Mifflin, 1896), pl. H. Page: H. 9³⁄₁₆″, w. 6³⁄₄″. ¶ The color plates in this volume, by a member of a well-known family of sporting-goods manufacturers, are dazzling reminders of the golden age of dry fly-fishing.

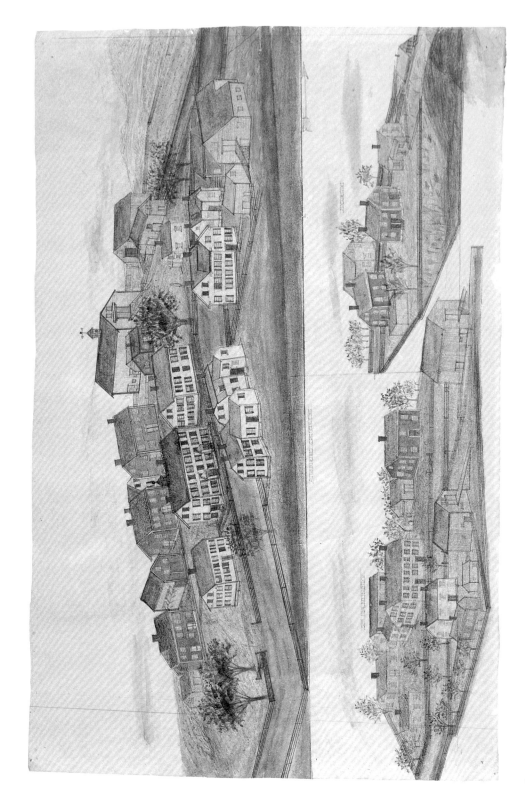

PLATE 12. Joshua Bussell, [*Alfred Shaker Community*], ca. 1850. Watercolor; H. 19¼", W. 29". ¶ The artist who painted this watercolor was a cobbler by trade and an elder in the Shaker community in Alfred, Maine. Even though he had no formal artistic training, Bussell made watercolor documentary records, or what he called "plans," of Shaker villages in New England. In these works Bussell typically noted the layout of a community, the location of its roads, and the appearance of its nearby fields.

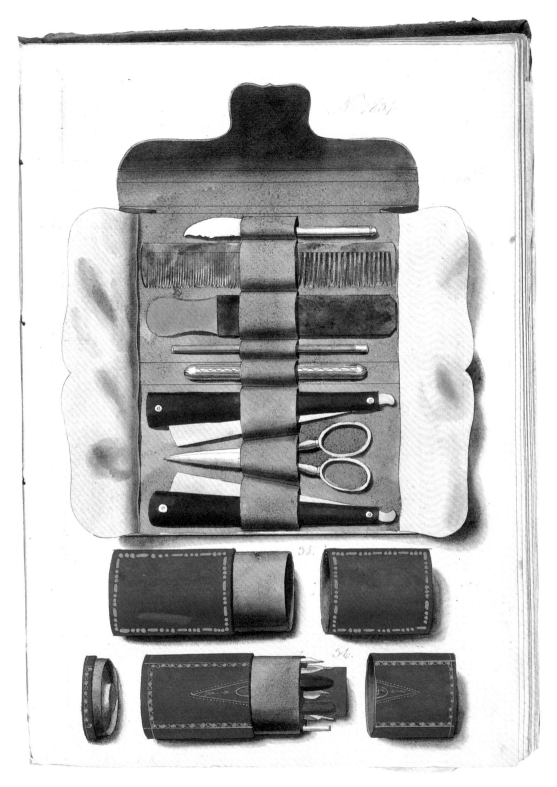

PLATE 13. Case with personal utensils. From [*Catalogue of Watercolor Drawings Depicting French Wares*], vol. 4 (France, [ca. 1810]), p. [67]. Page: H. 16″, W. 11″. ¶ This striking multivolume catalogue of watercolor drawings shows personal goods, chiefly life size, available to residents of France during the first decade of the nineteenth century. Probably used by an itinerant peddler, this catalogue is a remarkable document not only because of the items it includes but also because of its extraordinary artwork. Even though the products depicted are French, similar goods were shipped abroad and used in the United States.

De Schoenmaker.

PLATE 14. "De Schoenmaker." From *Geheel Nieuw Groot en Vermakelizk Prentenboek voor Kinderen* (Zalt-Bommel, Netherlands: Johannes Noman, 1826), facing p. [14]. Page: H. 9¾″, W. 8¼″. ¶ Although few have such superb illustrations, works such as *Geheel Nieuw Groot en Vermakelizk* were intended to acquaint children with the trades. Note the realistic details of this engraving, such as the wooden shoes in the rack on the wall.

Brawn on Stone by John French

Lith. of T. Sinclair Phil.

CITY HALL.
Built 1797

PLATE 15. "City Hall." From John Collins, *Views of the City of Burlington, New Jersey . . . Taken from Original Sketches* (Burlington, 1847), pl. [1]. Page: H. 9½", W. 12". ¶ A lithographer and watercolor artist active from the 1830s through the 1860s, John Collins was working in Philadelphia with lithographer Thomas Sinclair when this volume was published. Sinclair's name appears at the bottom of the plate. Another co-worker, Pennsylvania-born John T. French, is credited with actually drawing the scene on stone. Collins's relatively small book of village scenes contains fourteen plates showing city hall, private residences, churches, and St. Mary's Hall, a private school still in operation. Collins is also responsible for similar illustrated works on Philadelphia and Newport, Rhode Island.

PLATE 16. Karl Bodmer, "Matò-Tope / A Mandan Chief." From Maximilian Alexander Philipp, Prinz von Wied-Neuwied, *Reise in das Innere Nord-America* . . . (Coblenz: J. Hoelscher, 1839–41), pl. [3]. Page: H. 24″, w. 17½″.
¶ From 1832 to 1834, Karl Bodmer traveled the United States from Massachusetts to Montana with Maximilian, a German nobleman. The prince hoped to compile a work that reflected his interest in "the rude, primitive character of the natural face of North America, and its aboriginal population, the traces of which are now scarcely discernible in most parts of the United States" (quoted in Friends of Winterthur, *Annual Report* [Winterthur, 1964], p. 27). This provocative portrait of Matò-Tope in full feathered headdress is one of Bodmer's eighty-one engraved landscapes, towns, and portraits.

Foreword

Housing nearly half a million manuscripts, printed items, and visual images, Winterthur Library, established in 1951 with material collected by Henry Francis du Pont, is a research center for the interdisciplinary study of American art, material culture, and history. The strength of the library's collections resides in three areas: materials that describe the design, production, marketing, and use of American domestic objects and the foreign models and antecedents on which many of them are based; materials that record and illustrate American art and architecture; and materials that document everyday life in America from its beginnings into the twentieth century. Given the variety of items in the library's collections—rare printed books, manuscripts, pamphlets, advertising ephemera, and visual materials, to name just a few—*American Cornucopia* is an appropriate title for a book about Winterthur Library.

From its earliest years, Winterthur's staff devoted much attention and energy to building a library capable of supporting advanced research. Henry Francis du Pont's vision and devotion fired the minds of those charged with developing the library, and each left his or her own mark. Helen R. Belknap presided over the Memorial Library housed in the museum. The Memorial Library, which contained du Pont's personal collection of books and manuscripts, provided the nucleus of the library's collections today. Having demonstrated its importance to staff, visitors, and students in the then newly established Winterthur Program in Early American Culture, the library was moved to the Louise du Pont Crowninshield Research Building in 1969 so that the collections would have room to grow. In the same period, two dedicated volunteers, Mr. and Mrs. John J. Evans, Jr., developed the library's extraordinary collection of photographs documenting American decorative arts. This collection now numbers more than 150,000 images and is recognized as an essential resource for research projects in the American decorative arts.

The library has also been influenced by an archaeological approach to collecting introduced by Frank H. Sommer III. From 1963 when he was appointed head of the library until his retirement in 1988, Sommer's passion for acquiring as many types of materials on a subject as possible resulted in collections of encyclopedic breadth. His interest was piqued both by works whose importance was widely recognized and by the seemingly insubstantial. Sommer collected not only leather-bound rare books but also valentines, not only architectural drawings but also seed packets. Because Sommer found merit in all sorts of verbal and visual records and did not classify these materials hierarchically by their perceived importance or potential usefulness, Winterthur Library gained a reputation as a pioneering institution in focusing attention on the lives of anonymous people, particularly on domestic life, an unfashionable subject among historians of the 1950s and early 1960s. As a result of Sommer's efforts, social and economic historians are now more likely to research and base their conclusions on materials such as paper dolls, scrapbooks, or the records of a general store, a blacksmith, or a jeweler.

For the library staff, the satisfaction of helping researchers is enhanced by the pleasure of discovering and rediscovering treasures throughout the collections. Writing the present volume was an additional pleasure, for it allowed us to explore individual areas of interest to a degree difficult to achieve in the normal course of duty. It also provided an opportunity to exhibit items that are only occasionally seen because their sensitivity to light precludes displaying them even briefly at public exhibitions. Finally, writing this book has been a pleasure because it allowed us to call attention to some of our recent acquisitions. Winterthur's staff, students, and visitors are already well aware that the library houses great riches, in part due to the continuing support of the Friends of Winterthur and the Waldron Phoenix Belknap Trust. Yet as the collections continue to grow, the arrival of a rare woodworking manual or a volume of fabric swatches may go unnoticed. I hope that *American Cornucopia* will offer some surprises to even our most seasoned users, as well as an overview of the collections and the opportunities the library offers for research. To serve these needs, *American Cornucopia* was produced.

Katharine Martinez

Architecture

Much of the fascination of architectural history lies in what the clash and intermingling of theory and practice reveal about a period. The great literature of Western architectural theory begins with classical theorists such as first century B.C. architect Vitruvius. For several centuries, his writings stood unchallenged as the bedrock of Western architectural theory and still remain essential for an understanding of buildings of the past. Vitruvius and his fellow classical theorists never stood alone, however; Gothic and Oriental modes have often had apologists. In addition, maverick and highly personal theories about building have always found expression, a notable American example being the polemics of Orson Squire Fowler, originator of the octagon house.

Vitruvius and Fowler represent architectural writing at its most theoretical; however, architectural literature concerns much more than theory. As anyone who attempts to document the history of a building soon learns, a vast range of supporting material can shed light on its history, including books on building methods, old postcards and photographs, price books, insurance and tax records, wills and deeds, local histories, newspaper articles, drawings, and other manuscript material. Such sources are essential for explaining the actual appearance and condition of a structure as it changes over time, for few man-made artifacts are altered so often and so visibly as buildings. Vernacular and modest structures are particularly difficult to understand and interpret without such supporting materials since frequently little or no documentation exists by the builders or original owners.

Winterthur Library is particularly rich in the theoretical and prescriptive writings that have profoundly shaped Western architectural traditions. The library holds key early works such as Bartoli's 1550 translation of Alberti, the first illustrated edition of this important early writer; Barbaro's 1556 translation of Vitruvius into Italian; and the 1563[?] Rome edition of the masterwork of Giacomo Barozzi, better known as Giacomo da Vignola. Because Winterthur's copy of this last work contains five additional plates, it is as important as an artifact as it is as a source of information. Reflecting the quickened pace of architectural publication in the seventeenth and later centuries, the library's collection of theoretical works

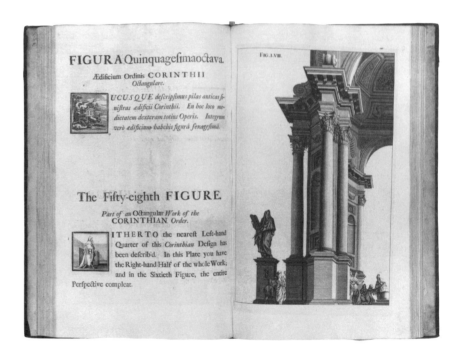

Fig. 1. "Part of an Octangular Work of the Corinthian Order." From Andrea dal Pozzo, *Rules and Examples of Perspective Proper for Painters and Architects* . . . , trans. J. Sturt (London: J. Senex and R. Gosling; W. Innys; J. Osborn and T. Longman, [170?]), fig. 58. Page: H. 16″, W. 10″.

While the illustrations in this English translation of Pozzo's work (originally published in Rome in 1693) are handsome in themselves, they had a more serious purpose than decoration. According to Pozzo's translator, Sturt, a thorough command of perspective was essential to the proper understanding of architecture and the sister arts. Pozzo's dramatic style of rendering perfectly matches its subject. Perhaps the most impressively endorsed architectural book ever published, *Rules and Examples* contains a testimonial signed "Chr. Wren, J. Vanbrugh, & N. Hawksmoor."

from later eras is larger, with editions of Vincenzo Scamozzi, Ferdinando Galli da Bibiena, Roland Fréart de Chambray, Jan Vredeman de Vries, perspectivist Andrea dal Pozzo (fig. 1), and others. But the library's most impressive holdings are architectural works from Great Britain. Spanning publications from the first English-language editions of Palladio (1715) and Alberti (1726), through builders' guides of the eighteenth century, to the influential "villa books" of James Malton, Peter Frederick Robinson, and their early nineteenth-century contemporaries, the library's collection of architectural works from Great Britain has a remarkable breadth and depth. Certain of the library's titles are rare or unique. Robert and James Adam's *Works in Architecture*, for example, has hand-colored plates, and Stephen Riou's *Grecian Order of Architecture* and elder John Wood's *Description of the Exchange of Bristol* are annotated by their authors. What is especially valuable about the library's collection of theoretical works on British architecture, though, is the assemblage of so many titles in one place, especially since so many appeared in editions of only a few hundred. The American counterparts of these works are here as well, from the very first architectural work published in this country—Abraham Swan's *British Architect* (1775)—through the manifestos of Gustave Stickley, a prominent leader of the arts and crafts movement.

Much of the meat of architectural publication, however, is practical rather than theoretical. Extremely popular in nineteenth-century America, house pattern books, such as Samuel Sloan's *Model Architect*, provided

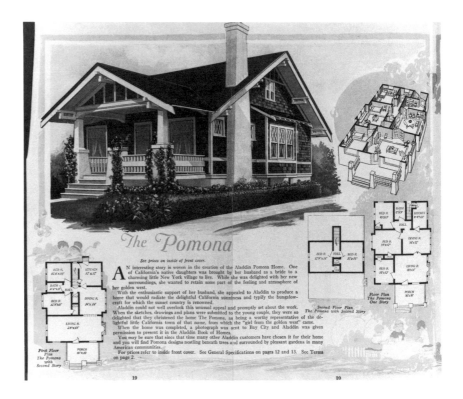

Fig. 2. "The Pomona." From Aladdin Company, *Aladdin Homes: "Built in a Day"* (Bay City, Mich., 1919), pp. 19–20. Page: H. 8³⁄₁₆″, W. 9¾″.

Aladdin Company's attractive catalogues are interesting for the manner in which houses are presented, each in a capsule short story. Respectability was evidently a major concern for a company marketing a building type still regarded with suspicion by conservative buyers.

builders with specifications and directions for constructing houses and advertised mail-order homes. As indicated by Aladdin Company's 1919 catalogue of homes, an entire fabricated dwelling could be bought by post and erected on the purchaser's site (fig. 2). As early as the eighteenth century, however, associations of house carpenters issued builders' guides and handbooks for particularly difficult construction jobs such as fireplaces and staircases. Nicholas Gauger's *Fires Improv'd* (1715), based on his earlier *Mécanique du feu* (1713), is an early example.

As demonstrated by Thomas Tredgold's *Practical Essay on the Strength of Cast Iron and Other Materials* (1824), new technologies and materials in the nineteenth century led to greater specialization in the literature of building. Trade catalogues for manufactured building elements also appeared at this time, the iron store fronts featured in the catalogue for Mesker and Brother providing a handsome example (fig. 3). Printed works in fields ancillary to architecture—landscape gardening, city planning, and early archaeological surveys—are represented in the library as well.

Architectural drawings and related manuscript sources are among the most personal expressions of an architect's intentions. The library's collection of drawings for domestic architecture includes a group of renderings (as well as letters and even a rudimentary treatise) by important

29

Fig. 3. Cover, Mesker and Brother, *Architectural Catalogue [of] Galvanized Iron Work* (St. Louis, Mo., 1888). H. 12⅛″, W. 9⅝″.

Mesker and Brother's *Architectural Catalogue* is as handsomely produced as its cast-iron building elements. Both catalogue and buildings are equally expressive of an age that delighted in ornament.

nineteenth-century architect Alexander Jackson Davis; a detailed set of plans and elevations for an 1840s town house for the Skidmore family of Brooklyn by Thomas Thomas; late eighteenth-century watercolors by Benjamin Henry Latrobe's first American pupil, Frederick Graff (and Graff's own annotated copy of Latrobe's report on the Philadelphia waterworks); and Nicholas King's charming plan and perspective of a dwelling for the city of Washington, dated 1798 (pl. 1). An important group of materials recently acquired by the library is the working papers, drawings, and research notes of distinguished restoration architect G. Edwin Brumbaugh. Brumbaugh's papers bear on many aspects of architectural research, especially on eighteenth-century Pennsylvania architecture.

The library's collection of architectural works is, of course, invaluable to curators and other staff members who care for old structures, but it is also vitally important to scholars devoted to studying the history and application of design. Consequently, Winterthur Library houses a broad range of materials to provide scholars with the background necessary for a thorough appreciation of architectural theory and practice.

Ornament

Fig. 4. Ornament designs from Alexis Loir, [*Suite of Ornament Etchings*] (Paris: N. Langlois, [ca. 1700]), pl. 3 designs 6–10. Page: H. 12¹¹⁄₁₆″, W. 7½″.

Designer Loir provides a visual encyclopedia of motifs based on natural forms that could be adapted to carved furniture, wall coverings, and applied decoration.

Who can resist the urge to decorate a plain surface? Until quite recently, skilled craftsmen, architects, and designers were well versed in an extensive vocabulary of decorative motifs, including fleurons, scrolls, grotesques, festoons, arabesques, and volutes. Alexis Loir's suite of ornament etchings illustrates a few of the many traditional design motifs used by artisans of earlier ages (fig. 4). Because ornament designers often recorded their work on paper, scholars today can trace the derivation and subsequent evolution of the ornament found on decorative objects by studying the publication history of printed ornament.

The impetus for much subsequent European ornamental decoration began in Italy during the Renaissance. The rediscovery of ancient Roman architecture together with the invention of printing stimulated the development of an Italian vocabulary for both structural and surface decoration that spread throughout Europe. Roman architectural elements such as columns and friezes became the chief elements in the classical vocabulary for structural decoration, whether in buildings or in furniture. At the same time, the wall decorations discovered during the excavation of Emperor Nero's *Domus Aurea* in 1488 gave rise to a playfully animated style of surface decoration called grotesque in reference to the underground grottos in which the wall decorations were discovered. From these sources European ornament evolved.

Ornament prints issued in portfolios or suites served as disposable paper patterns that could be easily handled, cut up, and copied before being thrown away. Indeed, the ephemerality of these images accounts for their modern rarity. The titles given to suites of ornament prints, such as *A Compleat Book of Ornaments . . . Being Very Useful for Painters, Carvers, Watchmakers, Gravers*, usually emphasize the usefulness of the plates for a variety of projects. As the above title and Paul Androuet Ducerceau's designs show, a single design could be applied to many surfaces (fig. 5).

By the eighteenth century, ornament prints were widely popular not only among professional craftsmen and architects but also among connoisseurs, collectors, and leisured upper-class ladies seeking designs to copy in needlework. Typically, eighteenth-century ornament etchings were

Fig. 5. Ornament design from Paul Androuet Ducerceau, *Ornement servant aux brodeur ouvrier en soie et orfevre et autre* (Paris, [ca. 1660–1710]), pl. 1. Page: H. 8″, W. 11″.

Ducerceau (ca. 1630–1713), a designer and goldsmith, was known for his scrolling foliage patterns. In this example, he presents a repeating pattern. If each end of the paper were brought together to form a circle, the pattern edges would fit together to create an unbroken, or repeating, scroll.

available singly or in suites that contained six to twelve plates held together with simple stitches at the left edge, occasionally with a title sheet to attract buyers. The sheet size of the paper for such a suite was usually not large, although exceptions, such as Giovanni Ottaviani's *Loggie di Rafaele*, were made for artists who were universally admired. Jean Berain and Juste Aurèle Meissonier also had their work issued in folio size, as befitted designers holding the title "dessinateur de la chambre et du cabinet du roi," the highest honor bestowed on a French designer.

A suite of ornament prints might be devoted to a single motif, such as the cartouche in Friedrich Unteutsch's *Neues Zieratenbuch den schreinern Tischlern* (fig. 6), or combine a number of decorative motifs or patterns for specific objects, such as vases or chimneypieces. Often designers would illustrate a single object or motif with two different halves joined in the middle, in order to cram as many designs as possible onto the available sheets of paper. Although designs in a suite were usually not arranged in any particular hierarchical or sequential order, a lovely exception to this rule is Matthias Lock's *Principles of Ornament; or, The Youth's Guide to Drawing of Foliage.* For one shilling the buyer obtained a lesson in drawing leaves that become increasingly complex as one turns the pages until the design culminates in a rococo floriate scroll. Suites and single sheets of ornament designs were often bound together by publishers and booksellers or pasted into blank volumes by their owners. Winterthur

Library has several bound compilations and scrapbooks, including a volume belonging to English silver-plate manufacturer Matthew Boulton in its original French vellum binding. This compilation contains twelve suites of ornament designs, including ones by François Boucher, Jean-Antoine Watteau, and Claude Gillot.

Many factors contributed to the wide dissemination of ornament designs in Europe. Artists and designers such as Daniel Marot, Jean Le Pautre, and François de Cuvilliés traveled extensively between European courts and cities, leaving a paper trail of their work. Italian designer Gaetano Brunetti, for example, was in England in 1736 when he issued *Sixty Different Sorts of Ornaments*, one of the earliest rococo pattern books published in England, before he traveled on to Paris. Through such printed works, design historians can trace the spread of a particular style throughout Europe.

Reprints and even plagiarized versions of printed ornament also spread designs quickly, indicating a healthy market for potentially useful images. The fanciful rococo prints produced in Paris by Jean Mondon

Fig. 6. Cartouche design from Friedrich Unteutsch, *Neues Zieratenbuch den schreinern Tischlern . . .* (Nuremberg: Paulüs Fürsten, 1635), pl. 5. Page: H. 6½″, w. 4⅞″.

The designs of Friedrich Unteutsch (1600–1670), a German cabinetmaker, are auricular, a style modeled on the undulating shapes of earlobes or cartilage. Such forms most commonly appear in carved European furniture of the seventeenth century.

Fig. 7. "Die verliebte Zusamenstimung."
From Jean Mondon, *Neu Inventierte
Vorstellungen von Stein und Muschel
Werck mit Chinesischen Figuren verziert
Dritter-Theil* (Augsburg: Johannes
Georg Merz, [ca. 1750]), pl. M. Page:
H. 8⅝", W. 6½".

Mondon's fanciful tableau combines two important elements of rococo decoration: a play-
ful, elegant couple and a rocaille, an abstract,
asymmetrical shell.

during the 1730s were reprinted in Augsburg later in the century by a
publisher who was careful to include Mondon's name in each plate's imprint as the inventor of the designs (fig. 7). Other publishers were less
concerned about properly crediting their sources. London map and print
seller Robert Sayer published *A Collection of Figures and Conversations*
in 1771 based on the work of such French artists as Boucher and Claude-
Joseph Vernet. Sayer's vignettes served as sources for transfer-printed images on Wedgwood creamware as well as for Worcester porcelain. Clearly,
ceramics manufacturers did not care who originated a specific design as
long as they had a variety of attractive subjects to copy. London publisher
John Weale cared even less for accuracy. During the 1830s he rushed several volumes of ornament prints into circulation, claiming that all the designs in them were by Thomas Chippendale, when, in fact, they were by
Thomas Johnson and Matthias Lock.

Printed design sources were brought to America by the earliest
settlers. The 1687 inventory of Pennsbury Manor, the home of William
Penn, lists "1 paper boock of dutch draughts" in the "Joyners Roume"

(quoted in Benno M. Forman, "The Chest of Drawers in America, 1635–1730: The Origins of the Joined Chest of Drawers," *Winterthur Portfolio* 20, no. 1 [Spring 1985]: 26). Samuel Sympson's *New Book of Cyphers*, published in London in 1726, and John Guillim's *Display of Heraldry* of 1724 were also known to have served as models for American silversmiths. Occasionally, historians are lucky to find a design sketchbook signed by a known craftsman that demonstrates how American artisans developed their own ornament vocabulary. The library owns a student's book of watercolor designs for painted ornament executed from 1811 to 1812 by Christian Nestell, who later became an ornamental painter and gilder in Providence, Rhode Island (pl. 2). His designs are similar to those found in earlier English pattern books, such as *The Cabinet-Maker and Upholsterer's Drawing-Book* by Thomas Sheraton.

Instances of a direct link between an object's decoration and a printed pattern are very rare. Consequently, identifying a specific source for an object's ornament is difficult if not impossible in many instances. Although a pine wall bracket in Winterthur Museum is obviously based on a design for a girandole printed in Johnson's *One Hundred and Fifty New Designs*, the origin of other structural or applied decoration can seldom be pinpointed. The two most frequently cited sources for japanned decoration are John Stalker and George Parker's *Treatise on Japanning and Varnishing* and George Edwards and Matthias Darly's *New Book of Chinese Designs*. Yet japanned decoration may also be based on such sources as Francis Barlow's *Booke Containing Such Beasts as Are Most Usefull for such as Practice Drawing, Gravaeing, Armes Painting, Chaseing*; the work of another craftsman; or the maker's own sketches. That artisans created their own designs for japanned decoration is evident from a sketchbook in Winterthur Library dated approximately 1817–20. Attributed to an Englishman named H. Wrightson, the sketchbook includes drawings of flowers and animals, plus vignettes with oriental figures.

The importance of ornament prints in the design process is a continually fascinating subject for decorative arts scholars to ponder as they attempt to tease into place the links connecting artistic inspiration and finished product. The apparent lack of a direct connection between printed image and finished object challenges scholars to continue thumbing through volumes and portfolios of images in the attempt to discover missing links. Even when such direct links are not discoverable, ornament prints are a useful barometer of the market for a particular decorative style. Why would a publisher sink money into a publishing project that would not be lucrative? At the same time, ornament prints reflect the ever-changing tastes of craftsmen who avidly sought new ornament designs in order to respond to the public's demand for new material goods. In fact, the manner in which designers such as Loir, Ducerceau, Sayer, and Barlow crowded multiple motifs onto a single sheet encouraged constant change. The newest ornamental designs became passé very quickly. Fortunately for scholars, ornament prints capture and freeze onto paper a visual vocabulary that was then and is now in a perpetual state of flux.

Interiors

Documenting interiors and their furnishings is at the heart of Winterthur's mission. Because we often have incomplete records of the appearance of furnished rooms before the advent of photography, reconstructing them can call for a combination of many different sources and considerable detective work. Inventories, auction records, prints, illustrations, genre paintings, diaries, travel narratives, trade catalogues, and prescriptive works by designers and decorators all offer clues and are sought by the library.

While each of these sources provides important evidence for the look of a historic room, it is important to distinguish between those that prescribe the way a room should look and those that record interiors in which people actually lived. Prescriptive works often depict fashions that few could afford to duplicate exactly but from which many craftsmen and householders drew ideas. As experience demonstrates, few actual room settings are "all of a piece" through economic necessity or personal taste, and personal taste, however shaped, in the end dictates that no two rooms are ever exactly alike. For this reason, records of actual rooms—compiled through inventories, photographs, or sketches—are very useful. The inventory of the furnishings of George Washington's residence in New York tells us very precisely what the interiors contained and how much their furnishings were worth. Such inventories, combined with surviving examples of listed furnishings, are vital for recreating the contents of historic interiors. However, as one travels farther back in time, fewer and fewer such interiors have been preserved or recorded, especially those belonging to members of the middle and working classes. Consequently, reconstructing them poses a special challenge. Fortunately for students of American interiors, John Lewis Krimmel's watercolors of early nineteenth-century Pennsylvania interiors are very revealing (pl. 3).

Prints are another major source of information for the appearance of interiors. Among the prints most influential in their day were the suites of designs by Huguenot Daniel Marot (ca. 1663–1752), who brought the grand style of the French court to the Low Countries, where it then passed to England. Marot designed furniture, decoration, gardens, vases, upholstery, clocks, and tombs (fig. 8). So influential was Marot's work, in

Fig. 8. Interior in the William and Mary style. From Daniel Marot, *Werken* (Amsterdam, 1707), pl. 53. Page: H. 14⅛″, w. 9¼″.

Marot is a major figure in the history of interiors. His houses, furnishings, and gardens and the record of them preserved through his publications were enormously influential in forming what we now call the William and Mary style. This plate embodies some of the key elements of that style, most notably the assemblage of blue and-white china above the fireplace.

fact, that an early owner of the copy of *Werken* now at Winterthur compiled an index to it and inscribed the place and date it was acquired: "This book . . . was bought at Mr. Robt. Freebairn's auction . . . Feb. 1709."

By the end of the eighteenth century, neoclassical style prevailed in Europe and this country alike. Because it was adaptable to many places and situations, neoclassical style was spread by a variety of publications, including fashionable magazines such as Rudolph Ackermann's *Repository of Arts*. While the influence of Ackermann's journal has long been acknowledged, other magazines with exquisite illustrations such as *Magazzino di Mobilia* from Italy and *Magazin für Freunde des guten Geschmacks* from Germany helped to spread interior decoration and furnishings in the Pompeian, Egyptian, and even the Gothic styles, which were also fashionable (pl. 4). Works such as George Smith's *Collection of Designs for Household Furniture* were responsible for popularizing styles among the affluent. On the other hand, two English auction catalogues in the library, both dated 1803, reveal through their room-by-room lists of household contents how interiors were actually furnished. Although the contents of a property auctioned by a man named Terry belonged to a "farmer and corn-dealer," and those of one auctioned by Henshaw belonged to Sir George Chetwynd, baronet, the neat mahogany chairs and handsome Pembroke tables found in the drawing rooms of both houses bear a remarkable similarity. Authentic settings are also discoverable in the library's set of 1830s watercolors by an amateur artist named Louisa Clinton. Her sketches of chairs and tables set in what are probably Scottish country homes demonstrate the importance of artifacts placed in relation to specific places, times, and circumstances.

During the nineteenth century, a great variety of period interior styles proliferated, spread in part by the increasing number of design publications. A taste for rococo revival appears in the 1840 *House Decorator and Painter's Guide*, a sort of trade catalogue issued by H. W. and A. Arrowsmith, "decorators to Her Majesty." Interiors illustrated in this work were only for the few who could afford the cost and sought the novelty of change. Like that of the Arrowsmiths' guide, the primary purpose of *Suggestions for Household Decoration* by London firm T. Knight and Sons was to advertise its decorating services for a prosperous clientele. Nevertheless, *Suggestions* is a marvelous compendium of period interiors, in which the new "aesthetic" taste meets and mingles with elements from other eras. The contents of a New York town house of the 1860s auctioned by J. L. Vandewater fills out the picture of design in the nineteenth century by suggesting how the influx of styles affected consumers. The Vandewater auction catalogue indicates, for example, that the owner of the town house had purchased his piano from Bacon and Raven and his "new and original Mexican oil painting" from the Art Union, the latter at a cost of $200. The nineteenth century also saw significant numbers of women writers enter the field of decoration and its literature. A modest amateur contribution, Eliza T. Van Schaack's *Woman's Hand*, narrated the story of a cobbler's wife who confounded her country neighbors by transforming her humble cottage with her hands and a little paint. Maria Richards Dewing, wife of an American painter, also wrote an advice book for the housewife-decorator, *Beauty in the Household*, which makes conscious claims for the civilizing mission of good household design.

Photography, of course, transformed the documentation of interiors, bringing to it an immediacy missing from previous sources, although in such "house books" as that of the beautifully photographed Smitley residence, the house is sitting for its portrait just as surely as its proud owner would have. Similar photographs exist for a now demolished cottage on the Winterthur grounds (fig. 9). A 1915 compendium of then-current taste, *The Room Beautiful* manages to capture a more international range of interiors at their best, as do the photographs of Biedler-Viken documenting the John Hay Witney house in Locust Valley, New York, in the 1940s. The impeccably conventional good taste of the latter contrasts

Fig. 9. Interior of Winterthur Cottage. Winterthur Cottage, photograph album, date unknown. Album: H. 7⁵/₁₆″, W. 9¼″.

Photography, often of very high quality, has preserved the look of a surprising number of mid to late nineteenth-century interiors, among them this now-vanished house on the du Pont estate.

with F. S. Lincoln's photographs of the Oyster Bay home of Bertha King Benkard, collector and close friend of H. F. du Pont's. Reflecting the assumptions and values of the heroic age of American collecting, the furnishings in the library's photographs of the Benkard house compare most appropriately with those depicted in Winterthur Archives' handsome drawings of room settings for du Pont. Executed by Leslie Potts, these watercolors are valuable both as documentation and as artifacts in their own right.

While viewpoints and interpretations may change with the tides of scholarship, inventories, auction catalogues, prints, genre paintings, design treatises, diaries, and deeds remain the essential raw materials from which all scholarship concerning interiors draws. The search for and acquisition of such sources is Winterthur Library's unchanging and very high priority.

Furniture

Fig. 10. Armchair, southeastern England, ca. 1690. From Robert Wemyss Symonds Collection, photographs and documents, ca. 1920–58, English furniture, ca. 1450–1850. Photograph: H. 11⅛", w. 8⅞".

Robert Wemyss Symonds, a remarkable English scholar and writer, built over many years an extensive research collection of photographs of privately and publicly owned furniture. This photograph of an elaborately carved armchair is one of several thousand documenting a wide stylistic and geographic range of English furniture forms. Symonds's correspondence and the annotations of his daughter Virginia who took voluminous notes on woodworking craftsmen from early newspapers and journals supplement the photographs, some of which were published in Symonds's articles and books. Since Winterthur Library acquired the Symonds Collection, American scholars have found studying English antecedents of American furniture much easier.

Since furniture can be fully understood only within the historical context provided by design manuals, artists' sketches, account books, receipts, and invoices, the symbiotic relationship between Winterthur Museum and Winterthur Library is, perhaps, most apparent in the study of furniture and related woodworking trades. However, while the museum's furniture collection is limited to American examples before 1860, the library's collection of materials concerning the history of furniture is international in scope and documents the full range of seventeenth-, eighteenth-, and nineteenth-century styles, plus the arts and crafts and colonial revival movements of the twentieth century.

Of course, the earliest American furniture was directly based on English and European pieces. Consequently, the Robert Wemyss Symonds Collection of photographs of early English furniture provides essential documentation for scholars who seek to locate a specific source for a piece of early American furniture or to understand the influence of English traditions on American craftsmanship (fig. 10). In addition to finding inspiration in actual European examples, American furniture craftsmen found ideas for their work in English and Continental pattern books, although they inevitably reshaped the designs illustrated in such publications in light of their individual training, the availability of materials and technologies, and the expectations of their customers. André-Charles Boulle's *Nouveaux deisseins de meubles et ouvrages de bronze et de marqueterie*, John Crunden's *Joyner and Cabinet-Maker's Darling*, Thomas Milton's *Chimney-piece-Maker's Daily Assistant*, Filippo Passarini's *Nouve inventioni d'ornamenti d'archittetura*, Thomas Chippendale's *Gentleman and Cabinet-Maker's Director*, and William Chambers's *Designs of Chinese Buildings, Furniture, Dresses, Machines, and Utensils* are just a few of the library's useful pattern books.

As important as European examples and pattern books in shaping the work of American furniture makers were foreign periodicals that published illustrations of and commentaries on the latest and most fashionable household furnishings. Because such journals are ephemeral, researchers at the library are fortunate to have issues of Pierre de La Mésangère's *Collection des meubles et objets de goût*, Rudolph Ackermann's *Repository* of Arts, Désiré Guilmard's *Garde-meuble, ancien et moderne*, and the *Magazzino di mobilia o sieno modelli di mobili di ogni genere*.

More directly related to American furniture history than either European pattern books or periodicals are the library's price books. Published in London, New York, Philadelphia, and Cincinnati, these works provided craftsmen with practical information on contemporary designs, local prices, and workmen's wages. *The Journeymen Cabinet and Chairmakers' New-York Book of Prices*, for example, indicates that a standard six-foot sofa with six legs could be customized. Consumers could order a longer sofa, add one or more legs or rails, or request removable arms or backs—each of these variations commanding a specific price. Of special interest to nineteenth-century furniture scholars is the *Book of Prices of the United Society of Journeymen Cabinet Makers*, published in Cincinnati in 1836, which illustrates many forms of the newly popular empire and neoclassical styles and provides patterns for craftsmen to follow.

Another essential aspect of the history of American furniture involves the original design drawings and notes of cabinetmakers themselves. Although such notes and drawings seldom survive, Winterthur Library has acquired a representative selection in its collection. Typical of the work of sophisticated urban craftsmen are the marvelous ink-and-watercolor drawings of William Gomm, an English cabinetmaker and upholsterer working in London at Newcastle House, Clerkenwell Close. William Gomm and Sons' "Sundry Drawings," dating between 1755 and 1763, show a variety of rococo furniture and interiors that demonstrate familiarity with the published designs of Thomas Chippendale, Thomas Johnson, and Lock and Copland. Although some of the furniture pieces illustrated in these drawings are plain and utilitarian, others have elaborate Gothic and Chinese designs (fig. 11). The Gomms' sophisticated furniture contrasts markedly with the rustic furniture depicted in the watercolor designs of T. Rutter of Lovegrove and Kennington Green. Beginning in 1819, Rutter designed and built summerhouses, garden seats, grotto baskets, flower stands, and venetian blinds. The popularity of rustic furniture is evident from the number of published works on the subject. Among the more significant in the library are *Ideas for Rustic Furniture* published in London in the 1780s and Johann Grohmann's *Recueil d'idées nouvelles pour la décoration des jardins et des parcs* published in Paris in 1796. Persistence of the style may be demonstrated by *Rustic Old Hickory Chairs, Rockers, Settees, Tables*, a 1902 trade catalogue by Old Hickory Chair Company of Martinsville, Indiana, which manufactured rustic furniture from 1899 to 1968.

Design drawings by American cabinetmakers provide insight into American furniture by revealing how American craftsmen adapted stan-

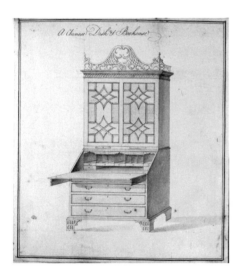

Fig. 11. *A Chinese Desk and Bookcase.* Drawing; H. 11⅛″, W. 9⅞″. From William Gomm and Sons, "Sundry Drawings of Cabinet Ware &c.," London, 1755–63.

The ink-and-wash drawings of William Gomm (ca. 1698–1794) depict various furniture forms and furniture in rooms. Furniture and interior decoration imaginatively adapted from Chinese models were fashionable in England, on the Continent, and in the United States in the second half of the eighteenth century.

dard forms to their own needs and when various styles came into and went out of fashion. Illustrating precisely measured and described eighteenth-century furniture, five ink drawings in the library show Daniel Arnd and Peter Ranck, Pennsylvania German craftsmen of Lancaster and Jonestown, translating popular Philadelphia designs into ones better suited to the small towns of eastern Pennsylvania. And pencil sketches of a lyre-back chair and a Grecian cross-front chair by Duncan Phyfe, the owner of a fashionable furniture shop in New York during the early nineteenth century, provide early American documentation of the "antique" style so popular in England. Phyfe's drawings apparently were sent circa 1816 to Charles N. Bancker, a Philadelphia customer, to illustrate Phyfe's new forms and to provide prices for them. A more detailed perspective of Phyfe in American furniture history can be gained through other resources in the library: Phyfe's own copy of *The New-York Revised Prices for Manufacturing Cabinet and Chair Work*; the auction catalogue for the sale of the entire stock of Duncan Phyfe and Son in 1847; and the 1854 inventory of the Duncan Phyfe estate.

Account books and other business records are also invaluable tools for research into American furniture, in large part because they document the materials that craftsmen purchased, the price paid for them and labor, and sometimes even the steps involved in producing a piece of furniture. They also reveal the price at which craftsmen sold their products and often information about the life-styles and values of craftsmen and their customers. The 1763–77 receipt book of Benjamin Randolph, an important eighteenth-century Philadelphia cabinetmaker, records that he purchased and had shipped oak, walnut, and mahogany lumber. The estate inventory of Michael Allison, on the other hand, lists finished pieces of furniture items and their market values—"Rosewood dressing bureau $30," "antique Looking glass $3," "Mahogany dining extension table $25"—thus supplying both an inventory of an actual home and a price index to furniture in New York in the 1850s. Another source of information about craftsmen and their practices is the trade card, the most graphic of which advertised William Buttre's "Fancy Chair Manufactory" in New York between 1805 and 1813 (fig. 12).

The account books of the Dominy family of East Hampton, New York, provide especially complete information about the activities of rural furniture makers since they cover three generations of cabinet- and clockmakers from 1762 until 1847. A sustained business record remarkable for its detail, the account books show that Nathaniel Dominy IV (1737–1812), Nathaniel Dominy V (1770–1852), and Felix Dominy (1800–1868) constructed a wide range of furniture forms for their clientele. They also made and repaired watches and clocks and performed cop-

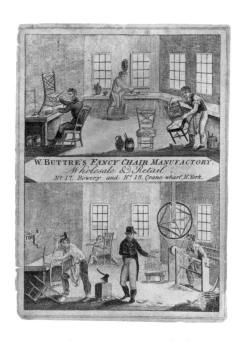

Fig. 12. William Buttre, trade card, New York, ca. 1813.

One of the most visually descriptive images in the library is this engraved trade card for the Buttre's Fancy Chair Manufactory. Virtually the entire chairmaking process is shown, starting at the lower right with a craftsman turning parts on a lathe, continuing with chair construction and rush-seat weaving at the lower left, and concluding with ornamental painting in the upper left. Buttre's address in New York indicates that the card was made circa 1813, before he moved upstate to Albany.

per-, black-, and gunsmithing as well. Complementing the library's collection are the museum's original Dominy workshops, tools, and furniture.

Probably no item in Winterthur Library, however, surpasses in historical interest George Washington's handwritten list of furnishings for the official residences of the president in New York and Philadelphia between 1789 and 1796. This manuscript records purchases from many of America's most prominent craftsmen such as Thomas Burling who made a bedstead, a writing desk, chairs, and "a table for Mrs. Washington"; Alexander McComb who sold an "Elegant chandelier" to the president; George Barteau (or Bartow) who upholstered two chairs and two stools; James Reynolds who provided picture frames; and James Dunlap who sold Washington looking glasses. In addition to these purchases, Washington carefully notes china, eating utensils, lighting devices, carpets, Franklin stoves, and other household items. Besides documenting the furnishings of the presidential residences, this list provides clues to Washington's personality and tastes.

The library collections for twentieth-century furniture are rich and varied. As important for its era as the Dominy Collection is for the nineteenth century, the Stickley Collection contains images and documents pertaining to Gustave Stickley, a leading figure in the arts and crafts movement. A furniture designer and manufacturer as well as the publisher of the *Craftsman*, a monthly periodical promoting the ideals of twentieth-century handicraft, Stickley was an influential entrepreneur. Winterthur Library houses 675 glass-plate photographic negatives illustrating various

Fig. 13. Sideboard, Craftsman Workshops, ca. 1905. From Gustave Stickley glass-plate negatives (and modern contact prints), furniture in Craftsman Workshops, Inc., Eastwood, N.Y., ca. 1905–16. Negative: H. 8″, W. 10″.

Printed from a glass-plate negative made for Stickley's furniture catalogues and books, this photograph of a sideboard is representative of the library's significant resources on the American arts and crafts movement. Important because they record most of the forms manufactured by Stickley until his bankruptcy in 1916, these negatives are also of interest to scholars because they depict various accessories made for and sold by the company.

Fig. 14. Dining room, Pickering house, Salem, Mass., ca. 1910. From Mary Harrod Northend, glass-plate negatives, early New England decorative arts and architecture, ca. 1905–20. Negative: H. 8″, W. 10″.

Mary Northend of Salem began photographing historic buildings, their interiors, and early American decorative arts early in this century. Many of her photographs (and those of other photographers she hired) illustrate her own books on the colonial revival, including *Colonial Homes and Their Furnishings* (1912) and *Historic Homes of New England* (1914). Here Northend photographed a room in the Pickering house, which was built in 1660 for John Pickering on land which had formed part of the Governor's Field originally owned by John Endicott. When Northend wrote and published information on this house, it had been continuously owned in the Pickering family. Its eighteenth-century chairs and portraits, nineteenth-century empire table, and twentieth-century "drugget" rug from India are typical of the family accumulations that appear in her photographs.

furniture forms made by Stickley's United Crafts enterprise at Eastwood, New York (fig. 13). It also contains business papers, account books, sales ledgers, merchandise lists, and other items from United Crafts, the earlier partnership of Stickley and Simonds Company, and the rival firm of L. and J. G. Stickley, a furniture company started by two of Gustave's brothers.

Yet another of the library's materials documenting the history of American furniture is the group of photographs taken for Mary Harrod Northend's many books and articles on New England houses and their furnishings. What is especially interesting about Northend's illustrations is that they provide accurate glimpses of the past in the process of change. Northend had photographs taken, for example, of the Pickering house which had been in continuous use in the same family from the mid seventeenth century. Consequently, many of the photographs for her works depict rooms housing both early American furniture and more recent acquisitions (fig. 14). A glimpse of the past in the process of change can also be obtained in Henry H. Crapo's carefully painted watercolors, circa 1880, of the rooms of the William J. Rotch house of New Bedford, which was designed by Alexander Jackson Davis in 1848. Although furniture made by Davis is illustrated in many of Crapo's watercolors, the rooms painted by Crapo also contain more recently purchased furnishings (pl. 5).

In sum, many types of documents and artifacts, each forging its own special link in the chain of information, are necessary for a full understanding of the development of American furniture. For this reason, Winterthur Library is dedicated to collecting a vast array of materials related to American furniture and furniture history.

Ceramics and Glass

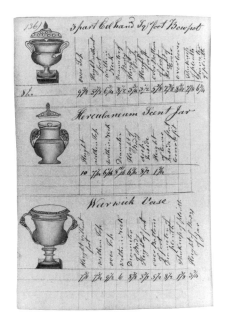

Fig. 15. "3 part Eel handd. Sqr. foot Bowfoot / Herculaneum Scent Jar / Warwick Vase." From Spode factory shape and pattern book, Stoke-on-Trent, Staffordshire, Eng., ca. 1815–21, p. 136. Page: H. 7⅞″, w. 5¾″.

Spode produced neoclassical forms such as the "Herculaneum Scent Jar" and the "Warwick Vase" to capitalize on the public's interest in the archaeology of Italy and the market for decorative accessories complementary to architectural interiors in the "antique" style. Tablewares including cups and saucers, tea- and coffeepots, and plates comprise the majority of design shapes in the pattern book, and precise measurements of each form are provided for production.

In a better world, cultural historians would be able to find all the craftsmen's designs, correspondence, account books, invoices, bills of lading, trade catalogues, and other artifacts needed to identify and understand American decorative arts. In reality, however, such resources are scarce, and scholars must often be detectives, piecing together history from scattered fragments of evidence.

Potters and glassmakers are among the least understood artisans because their craft is particularly hard to document. In contrast to silversmiths, cabinetmakers, clockmakers, and weavers, potters and glassmakers rarely marked their wares, which were produced in large quantities and sold at low prices to wholesale merchants or retail stores. Studying earthenware potters is especially difficult because many worked at their trade only part of the year to supplement farm income and do not appear as craftsmen on tax lists and census records. As a result, the surviving documentation for these elusive craftsmen and manufactories is extremely valuable.

Connoisseurship of ceramics is supported by design books and trade catalogues that describe or illustrate a particular manufacturer's products. Winterthur Library has a remarkable group of these reference works. One manuscript collected by H. F. du Pont records ceramics produced by the Spode Factory in Stoke-on-Trent, Staffordshire, England. English ceramics dealer, researcher, and writer Geoffrey A. Godden identified the manuscript in 1966 as a shape-pattern book for Spode's creamware and porcelain (fig. 15). Subsequently, numerous items at Winterthur and other American and British museums have been identified as Spode products. Another valuable manuscript pattern book in the library is that of Joseph Ball of Staffordshire, England, whose precise ink-and-watercolor drawings illustrate "Gaudy Dutch," "Gaudy Welsh," and luster-decorated wares exported to the United States in large quantities. Of slightly later date is *Illustrated Pattern Book*, an English china and glass wholesaler's catalogue that features the wares of many Staffordshire potteries, foreign porcelain makers, and European glass factories (pl. 6). Special because of its documentation of the international trade in ceramics in the mid to late nineteenth century is the two-volume *Catalogue Containing Watercolor*

Drawings of Japanese Porcelain, which illustrates fine porcelain and earthenware for export to the West (pl. 7).

American potters and manufactories are also well represented in the library's collections. The library holds pictorial billheads or price lists for Aldrich and McCormac (successors to C. M. Silsby and Company) in Troy, New Hampshire; N. Clark and Company in Lyons, Mount Morris, and Rochester, New York; and Fulper Brothers in Flemington, New Jersey, among others. In addition, the library contains trade catalogues whose accurate and appealing illustrations help to document wares of late nineteenth- and early twentieth-century potteries such as Rookwood Pottery in Cincinnati; Galloway Terra-Cotta Company in Philadelphia; and J. G. and J. F. Low in Chelsea, Massachusetts. The popular craft of china painting is documented by trade catalogues for companies providing porcelain firing kilns and enamel decorating colors, as well as original china-painting designs by such well known artists as Charles Volkmar (fig. 16).

The most fascinating resources for scholars of American pottery, however, are the few surviving daybooks of craftsmen. Their detailed descriptions of ware types, production dates, employee wages, and marketing strategies provide insights to the potter's craft and the relation of craftsmen to the community. The library's earliest daybook, which covers

Fig. 16. Charles Volkmar, *Perch*, 1894. Ink-and-watercolor on paper; H. 15⅝″, W. 12″.

Charles Volkmar (1841–1914) was an American artist equally adept in both the fine and the decorative arts. Trained in France as a painter and an etcher, Volkmar returned to the United States, working as an artist-potter in New Jersey and New York. When published, this ink drawing of perch in a lake was accompanied by instructions for adapting it to porcelain decoration. Many professional and amateur artists practiced china painting after the 1876 Centennial Exposition.

parts of 1761 and 1762, was recorded by Jeremiah Page, a brickmaker and seller in Danvers, Massachusetts. It documents sales of "hard bricks," "pale bricks," "well bricks," and tiles to customers throughout Essex County in exchange for goods or cash. The library also has daybooks by Samuel Swank, an earthenware potter located near Johnstown, Pennsylvania, and Christopher Fenton of United States Pottery at Bennington, Vermont. Covering the period between 1850 and 1857, Swank's book records sales to individuals and crockery dealers for a wide range of forms including "creamcrocks," "spittingboles," "smokepipes," "pie-dishes," and lamps. Fenton's daybook, on the other hand, documents the accounts payable for United States Pottery beginning April 14, 1847, listing purchases of wood, sand, plaster, "stone clay," and "fire clay," among other raw materials. In addition, it provides detailed notes on employees and their wages. The late nineteenth-century account ledger of John H. Sonner of Strasburg, Shenandoah County, Virginia, is intriguing for its depiction of a business failing over time due to changing technology. Sonner's ledger traces the diminishing trade in utilitarian stoneware as output and prices fell in competition with glass storage jars and bottles. To combat the trend, Sonner shared the time of master potter Theophilus Grim with other area potteries; employed his father, S. H. Sonner, as a handyman; and bartered his pottery for a wide variety of goods, including nails, a rocking chair, white lead, hams, tobacco, shingles, wood, sugar, and even his printing bills.

Because glass manufacture involves much more complex technology than ceramics, there were relatively few American glassmakers. Nevertheless, Winterthur Library contains important resources on glassware used and made in America. *Gardiners Island Glass Catalogue* may well be the library's most significant historical document on glass (fig. 17). Named for Gardiners Island, New York, where it was found, the two-volume catalogue has exquisitely clear ink-and-watercolor drawings of Bohemian glass that may represent the work of several glass manufactories. Scholars have found the first of its two volumes particularly useful in documenting early glass imported to the United States, much of which had hitherto been mistakenly attributed to American makers. Now this glass has been correctly identified with Bohemian manufacturers, largely because Johannes Schiefner, whose name appears on the "Preiss Courrent" accompanying each volume, is known to have been a glass merchant from Parchen, Bohemia. Evidently, Schiefner operated an export and commission agency in Russia, America, and Spain, among other countries.

American glass manufacture is revealed through many documents available in the library such as the account ledger kept by George Dummer of Jersey City Glass Works; the 1774 indenture between Henry Wil-

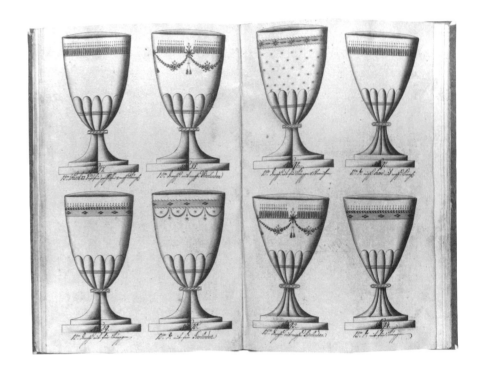

Fig. 17. Bohemian cut-glass goblets. From [*Gardiners Island Glass Catalogue*], vol. 1 (Gardiners Island, N.Y., [ca. 1805]), nos. 87–94. Wash and ink on paper; H. 14⅛″, w. 18″.

The clear ink-and-wash drawings of the glass catalogue illustrate and list prices for a wide variety of Bohemian tablewares and chandeliers exported to the United States in the late eighteenth and early nineteenth centuries. John Lyon Gardiner (1770–1816), the seventh proprietor of the island, may have been directly involved in the import trade.

liam Stiegel, a glass manufacturer, and Jeremias Miller, both of Manheim, Pennsylvania; and numerous receipts and illustrated billheads, including those for Orange County Flint Glass Works in Port Jervis; Boston Glass manufactory in Boston; and Bakewell, Pears, and Company in Pittsburgh. Of special note among the library's trade catalogues for American glass is one for Belcher Mosaic Glass Company of New York in 1886. Its unusual patented windows made of cast-lead frames and colored glass are illustrated with watercolor and printed designs, many in the popular Japanese style.

The pervasiveness of ceramics and glass in American culture ensures that researchers will continue to study primary documents to understand better many aspects of technology, cooking, eating and drinking, marketing and trade, interior decoration, and architecture. Winterthur Library is fortunate to have assembled such an extensive array of these rare research tools.

Metals

Printed and manuscript primary documentation is nowhere more valuable than in the metalworking trades, for very few examples except silver are signed or marked by a craftsman. Consequently, researchers in metalwork use trade catalogues, invoices, account books, and inventories to link artifacts to artisans. The library's extensive records of the business activities of silversmiths, brass founders, hardware importers, nailmakers, tinsmiths, engravers, clockmakers, jewelers, wheelwrights, and optical- and mathematical-instrument makers are therefore essential to identifying the makers of objects in Winterthur Museum's broad collections, from high-style silver of eighteenth-century Philadelphia, New York, and Boston to nineteenth-century imported brass and silver-plated wares and American utilitarian wrought-iron cooking implements. The library's materials on metals are also important in revealing the economic and social relations among craftsmen and the conditions of trade.

At the top of the hierarchy of craftsmen working in metal are goldsmiths and silversmiths, who provided the social elite, and later the middle class, with precious decorative and useful goods in the latest styles. Winterthur Library has such materials as commonplace books, letter books, and inventories from three generations of the Richardsons of Philadelphia, a prominent family of silversmiths working in the colonies. Francis Richardson (1681–1729) worked at his trade by age twenty in 1701. Richardson's account book is immensely valuable because it records his relations with Philadelphia craftsmen, including Johannis Nys, a fellow silversmith from whom he purchased goods; and Richard Keeble, who served as journeyman or master in Richardson's shop and from whom he later bought piecework. His account books also record exchanges of wrought silver and cash for chemicals, tools, coral, and bulk silver.

Both of Francis's sons, Francis, Jr. (1705–82), and Joseph (1711–84), were trained by their father and became silversmiths. Joseph's commonplace book provides a vivid description of his business transactions among Quaker craftsmen in eighteenth-century Philadelphia. Joseph's aesthetic and business relations are also indicated in the invoice book of Samuel Powel, a Philadelphia merchant, who records that Joseph requested him to purchase "an alphabet Cypher book to Engrave by [and] a book of Drafts to Draw by" during a 1724/25 trip to London.

When Joseph retired from the silversmith's trade, his two sons, Joseph, Jr. (1752–1831), and Nathaniel (1754–1827), inherited the family business. The younger Joseph's letter book for the years 1777–90 shows that he enjoyed a lively trade in imported scales and weights after the 1783 peace with England. Apparently, Philadelphians were demanding many other English goods as well, for an inventory of the shop of Joseph, Jr., and Nathaniel taken May 31, 1790, reveals a wide range of domestic and imported wares: "Salts with blue Glasses and Ladles," "pair Spurrs," "Pincushion chains," "Silver Whistles & Bells with Corals," "Egg Cups," "Toast Racks," and "15 pair box beam Scales in Shagreen cases."

Other highlights of the library's materials on American gold- and silversmiths include the Stanley B. Ineson Collection, which contains invoices for silver purchases, genealogical notes and data, photographs, drawings, and rubbings of silver marks compiled by Ineson, an early collector; the private letter book of Thomas Fletcher, which records the personal activities of this prominent Philadelphia silversmith and jeweler; and an account book of Jabez Baldwin, a Salem silversmith and merchant. Baldwin's account book illustrates particularly well the diversity required of colonial and federal gold and silversmiths who were expected to engrave, repair watches, make gold mounts for hair jewelry, and fashion sugar tongs, spoons, and hollowware. Baldwin's account book is also fascinating for its record of the stock owned by George Baker, who

Fig. 18. Lewis Deblois, trade card, Boston, 1757. Card: H. 6⅛″, W. 7⅜″.

The engraved trade card for Boston merchant Lewis Deblois is as notable for the skill and execution of its design as for its description of imported goods that Deblois sold. The Boston craftsman who engraved Deblois's card, Thomas Johnston (or Johnson, b. ca. 1708), was an engraver, portrait and heraldic painter, and "Japaner." The long list of goods Deblois imported "every Spring and Fall" indicates that although American manufacturers produced utilitarian iron- and brasswares, consumers still desired English fancy goods. Deblois used the back of this trade card as a receipt for a set of desk hardware that included brass drawer handles, escutcheons, locks, and hinges.

Fig. 19. Brass furniture hardware and household items. From [*Catalogue of Furniture Hardware and Sconces*] [Birmingham, Eng.?, ca. 1770], pl. 4. Page: H. 11¼″, w. 17½″.

This fold-out engraving of brass furniture hardware and related goods includes an elaborate rococo watch stand on a tripod base featuring a figure of Father Time amid putti, festoons, and scrollwork. As part of a trade catalogue for an unidentified Birmingham manufacturer, it provides an invaluable resource for the study of imported metalwares.

trained under Jabez Baldwin and worked in Salem and Providence. Among the items owned by Baker were a "Gold Watch Repeater" priced at $109.84, a set of English silverware at $100.00, a set of Philadelphia silverware at $117.25, a caster set with cut-glass bottles at $24.40, and a Britannia wine funnel at $1.40.

As the trade card for the shop of Lewis Deblois indicates (fig. 18), American merchants and craftsmen were as likely to import goods made of base metals as they were to import those of silver and gold. Among the more than thirty-five English pattern books at Winterthur concerning trade in base metals are two hardware catalogues originally owned by Samuel Rowland Fisher, a partner of Philadelphia mercantile firm Joshua Fisher and Sons. One contains saddlery and horse equipment sold by London firm Withers and Buchanan, as well as a manuscript list of prices charged for various styles of imported clock faces by John Wood. The second is an English brass founder's *Catalogue of Doorknobs, Escutcheons, Door Knockers, Furniture Brasses, Sconces, Etc.* Many of the designs illustrated in this catalogue were sold to Philadelphia cabinetmakers and may be matched with hardware on chests of drawers and other furniture in Winterthur Museum. Elaborate rococo designs fill yet another Birmingham catalogue of furniture hardware and sconces (fig. 19), while

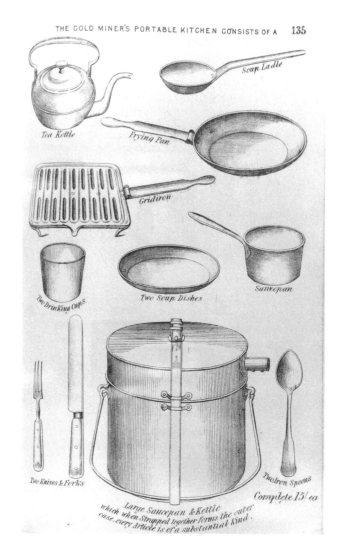

Fig. 20. "The Gold Miner's Portable Kitchen . . . ." From Griffiths and Browett, [*Catalogue*] (Birmingham, Eng., [ca. 1860]), p. 135. Page: H. 8½", W. 5¼".

As many Americans were journeying west in search of precious gold, England's metalwares industry sought its fortune in the base metals of tinplate and wrought and cast iron. In addition to offering this portable kitchen, Griffiths and Browett tempted Americans with a wonderful variety of goods including bathtubs and shower baths, grocers' showcases and canisters, and cake and jelly molds.

a wide range of utilitarian iron goods—including a "Gold Miner's Portable Kitchen" (fig. 20)—appears in the 1860 catalogue of Griffiths and Browett.

Like their English counterparts, American brass founders, coppersmiths, and manufactories are well represented in the library's collections. An illustrated billhead for John Bailey, a brass founder, a coppersmith, and an ironmonger in New York, depicts a federal-style andiron, brass kettle, fireplace fender, knifebox, and chamberstick. This billhead, which acknowledges Bailey's receipt of £5.5.0 for a pair of andirons, also documents Bailey's removal from 20 Little Dock Street to 60 Water Street. An 1892 catalogue for J. L. Mott Iron Works, New York, shows the wide variety of designs for copper and cast-iron weather vanes available from

COPPER WEATHER VANES.

GILDED WITH GOLD LEAF.

PLATE 40-Q.
DEER.
SWELL BODIED.
Price, 30 inches long, mounted complete with Spire,
Letters and Balls, ... $25 00

PLATE 41-Q.
POINTER DOG.
SWELL BODIED.
Price, 33 inches long, mounted complete with Spire,
Letters and Balls, ... $25 00

PLATE 42-Q.
SWAN.
SWELL BODIED.
Price, 27 inches long, mounted complete with Spire,
Letters and Balls, ... $40 00

PLATE 43-Q.
BOAR.
SWELL BODIED.
Price, 30 inches long, mounted complete with Spire,
Letters and Balls, ... $40 00

PLATE 44-Q.
BUFFALO.
SWELL BODIED.
Price, 36 inches long, mounted complete with Spire,
Letters and Balls, ... $65 00

PLATE 45-Q.
SETTER DOG.
SWELL BODIED.
Price, 36 inches long, mounted complete with Spire,
Letters and Balls, ... $25 00

Fig. 21. "Copper Weather Vanes." From J. L. Mott Iron Works, *Illustrated Catalogue "Q" and Price List: Vanes, Bannerets, Finials, &c.* (New York and Chicago, 1892), p. 22. Page: H. 11½", W. 9¼".

Among the finest American weather vanes of the nineteenth century are those from J. L. Mott Iron Works (established in 1828) of New York and Chicago. This 1892 catalogue, which illustrates and describes a wide variety of vehicles, figures, and animals, may assist scholars in identifying surviving works from this manufactory. The most elaborate patterns, such as Columbus, King Gambrinus, and a seven-foot-long steam fire engine with horses and driver, could cost as much as $250. The catalogue states, "We do not, however, limit ourselves to the manufacture of these designs only, but are prepared to give estimates on Architects' original designs, guaranteeing strictly first-class work at moderate prices."

this well-known manufacturer (fig. 21). A wide variety of designs is also evident in the work of Philadelphia coppersmith Robert Orr, whose trade card boasts, "Stills of all sizes: brewers, dyers, soap boilers, rope-makers, hatters, kettles, house pipes, ships stoves, etc."

Records of early American iron furnaces, forges, and blacksmiths are especially revealing about everyday life since they provide information about utilitarian goods, the active system of barter, and the industrial framework of the colonies and the early Republic. Account books for Berkshire Furnace, Berks County, Pennsylvania, record the sale of locks, skillets, a "½ Tun of Dutch Stoves," "700 [pounds of] Bare Iron," and "3 Tun Stoves." The credit side of the furnace's ledgers is just as fascinating as the debit one, for it shows the company exchanging goods for twenty-one pairs of shoes. Labor historians may also be interested to learn that in 1789, Michael Wood, an employee of Berkshire Furnace, was paid £20 for the services that his wife performed in keeping a company house

Fig. 22. George Christian Gebelein, *Hot-Water Kettle on Stand*, ca. 1915. Pencil, ink, transparent watercolor, and gouache on paper; H. 22″, W. 15″.

Foremost among American silversmiths of the early twentieth century was George Christian Gebelein (1878–1945) who opened his own shop in Boston in 1909. Gebelein is best known for crafting silver in the style of Paul Revere, Jr., and other early American makers, although he also worked silver in the hand-hammered style of the arts and crafts movement. This finished presentation drawing of a hot-water kettle on stand is one of the library's many fine examples of Gebelein's colonial revival work.

for the year. A strength of Winterthur Library's materials relating to American furnaces and forges is that its holdings cover a wide geographic range. The collections contain, for example, business records or accounts for Joseph Holmes Iron Works in Kingston, Massachusetts; Martick Iron Works in Smithburg, Pennsylvania; Ramapo Iron Works in Haverstraw, New York; and Trimble's Iron Works in an unidentifed Kentucky town.

Fortunately, the American colonial revival in the early decades of this century brought to early American handcrafted items and the artisans who made them much deserved recognition and appreciation. No doubt, some of the prestige that early American metalcrafts gained during this century was due to the influence of modern artisans such as George Christian Gebelein who brought the work of earlier generations to the attention of a broad modern audience. Gebelein of Boston, among this century's foremost silversmiths, based much of his work on prototypes by colonial silversmiths. The library has recently acquired many of Gebelein's preliminary sketches and presentation drawings for clients (fig. 22), thereby enhancing an already strong collection of manuscripts and photographs documenting early twentieth-century American metalworkers.

The unexpected diversity of the library's materials on the metalworking trades is epitomized by a rare hand-colored *Map of the Valley of the Sacramento including the Gold Region*. Published in Boston by T. Wiley, Jr., in 1848, it provided direction to many pioneer miners who flocked to California for gold, by instructing ship captains entering San Francisco Bay to "keep White Island open with the south shore and run for it within the harbor." In its reminder of the daunting 17,000 miles between New York and San Francisco via the Cape of Good Hope, the map inspires appreciation and respect for the products of American artisans working in metals.

Textiles and Needlework

Because textiles and needlework are highly perishable, information about their design, production, and use is elusive. A considerable body of literature describes textile design and manufacture by hand and by machine, but records of the use and appearance of actual fabrics in daily life are more difficult to come by and consequently more valued. Fortunately, some manufacturers' and retailers' swatch books, trade catalogues, and trade cards survive, as do relatively scarce instruction books for cutting and fitting household textiles and early photographs of clothes and interiors. However, such sources become progressively less common as one moves backward in time.

Fabric samples and swatches are vital primary documentation. Found in a surprising variety of sources, samples and swatches often retain their original, vivid colors. Such early nineteenth-century periodicals as Rudolph Ackermann's *Repository of Arts* and its German counterpart, the *Journal des Luxus und der Moden*, include tipped-in fabric samples advertising each nation's domestic manufactures. Other fabric samples are found in the library's extensive collection of swatch books, which sets forth the range of textile choices available to consumers in, among other times and places, mid nineteenth-century France and late eighteenth-century England. Such swatch books are valuable as well for the links they provide between obscure textile terms and the actual fabrics to which they refer. Yet other sources, such as trade catalogues, preserve samples of fabrics ranging from late nineteenth-century men's suiting to Shaker chair tapes. An early nineteenth-century instruction book for household needlework by the British and Foreign School Society contains actual examples of darning and hemming and even an exquisitely sewn baby's bonnet. The library's most extraordinary artifacts of fabric use and ownership, however, are the three scrapbooks assembled by Kate S. Harris of Salem County, New Jersey, in the 1880s. Here, carefully preserved and meticulously annotated, are scores of samples of clothing and furnishing textiles gathered from her own family and from those of friends and neighbors. One scrapbook is of wedding fabrics alone. As a group, Harris's scrapbooks form a most valuable record of fabric use at a specific time and place.

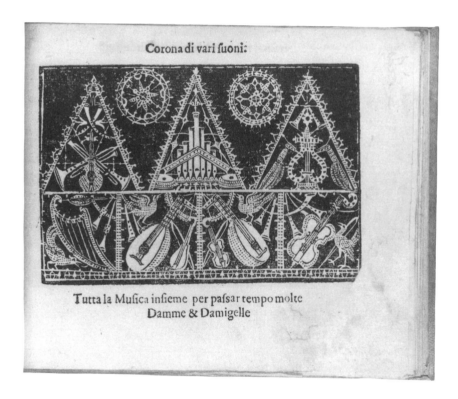

Fig. 23. "Corona di vari suoni." From Cesare Vecellio, *Corono delle nobili et virtuose donne . . .* (2d ed.; Venice, [1600–1625]), leaf [Bbb 6]. Page: H. 5¾", w. 7½".

This illustration depicts one leaf from a handsome collection of lace designs made in Venice, a city renowned for lacemaking for many centuries. Although Vecellio's *Corono* is one of the earliest printed pattern books for the handicrafts, it is among the most visually striking.

Scholars also learn about the uses of actual fabrics from printed books and photographs. While many handsome compilations contain countless variations of designs for window draperies or bed hangings, fewer sources can tell us just how such hangings were constructed. James Arrowsmith's *Analysis of Drapery* may lack the visual punch of its handsome contemporary, Pierre de La Mésangère's *Collection des meubles et objets de goût*, which contains plates of furniture and window hangings, but Arrowsmith's work is prized today for its scaled cutting diagrams and fabric measurement charts. A similar volume, John Saville Crofton's *London Upholsterer's Companion*, outlines the techniques of upholstery at the dawn of the great age of stuffing, from the viewpoint of a practitioner. Photographically illustrated trade catalogues from the later decades of the nineteenth century are useful because they record upholstered pieces as they actually appeared. Their importance for curator and conservator is obvious.

Although design books do not indicate directly how textiles were used, they help researchers to identify patterns and manufacturers. Design books for the textile arts have existed for centuries. One of the earliest in Winterthur Library is Cesare Vecellio's *Corono delle nobili et virtuose donne*, a collection of lace designs printed in Venice between 1600 and 1625 (fig. 23). Among the library's most spectacular design books is a full-color textile design album of paisleys, probably from early nineteenth-century France. Another design manuscript, also thought to be French, sets out a handloom weaver's draft designs for executing floral-pattern textiles. Fully colored and properly scaled finished designs appear on the same pages on which they were drafted (pl. 8). A manuscript design book of particular interest to Delawareans is the library's volume of calico patterns associated with the textile mill briefly operated on the Brandywine Creek near Wilmington by Irish political refugee Archibald Hamilton Rowan. While the venture failed, the designs themselves are lively and appealing.

Like their fellow textileworkers, embroiderers have turned to many sources for designs over the centuries. The charming woodcuts in Edward Topsell's *History of Four-Footed Beasts and Serpents* may be anatomically fanciful, but it provided popular embroidery patterns for many years (fig. 24). Much later, as nineteenth-century housewives stopped manufacturing

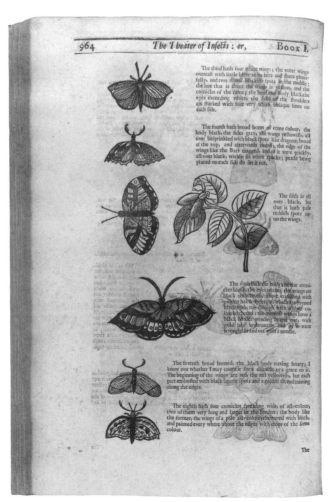

Fig. 24. Butterflies. From Edward Topsell, *The History of Four-Footed Beasts and Serpents . . . Whereunto Is Now Added, the Theatre of Insects . . . by T. Muffet . . .* (London: Printed by E. C., 1658), p. 964. Page: H. 13¼", w. 8¼".

Topsell's imaginative book of natural history included in this edition Thomas Muffet's similar work on insects, which was previously published separately. Muffet's work was in turn based on that of Conrad Gessner, a pioneer of natural-history illustration. Together, Topsell's and Muffet's studies became a classic source for subsequent illustrators and designers, including embroiderers, who would transfer motifs such as the butterflies shown here to fabric by pricking holes through the paper into a cloth below.

Fig. 25. Weaver's draft design, probably for a coverlet. From Johann Michael Frickinger, *Nützliches in lauter auserlesenen, wohl-approbirt- und meistentheils Neu-inventirten Mustern bestehendes, Weber-Bild-Buch . . .* (Neustadt and Leipzig: Jacob Samuel Friedrich Riedel, 1783), leaf [42]. Page: H. 9¼", W. 12".

Weavers' draft books, such as the one illustrated here, were brought to America by immigrant professional weavers and used well into the nineteenth century.

most textiles for their homes, a different sort of needlework book sprang up, containing detailed instructions for producing "fancywork" items such as pen wipers and hair receivers. The titles of these books, such as *Lonely Hours: A Text-book of Knitting*, by an American Lady, evoke the housewife's daily lot and the role that handwork played in filling her life.

Nineteenth-century trade cards and trade catalogues also provide valuable information about textiles. The library is especially fortunate in having a large collection of trade cards and catalogues for sewing machines, a technological miracle in the nineteenth century. Despite such technological breakthroughs, handloom weavers still traveled with looms and manuscript or printed drafts or patterns. One printed pattern book in the library is Johann Michael Frickinger's *Nützliches in lauter auserlesenen*, published in Leipzig in the eighteenth century. Tradition has it that Winterthur's copy was used in central Pennsylvania in the mid nineteenth century. The striking graphic quality of its weaving patterns seems quite contemporary today (fig. 25).

The textile and needlework documents discussed above, as well as others in Winterthur Library, share one quality: they are a pleasure to examine, tempting even the most disciplined researcher to abandon the collection of data and surrender to the sheer enjoyment of color and design.

Gardens

Winterthur Library's materials on landscape gardening consist of archival, printed, and manuscript works reflecting both the history of the du Pont family and the development of landscape design in America and Europe.

Henry Francis du Pont's interest in landscape gardening was whetted during the first two decades of the twentieth century. During this time, the garden at Winterthur became a testing ground for color in landscape design. To record his experiments with color, du Pont and his administrative assistant, H. B. McCollum, took some 400 images on glass between 1910 and 1916. This sumptuous collection of autochromes is now housed in Winterthur Archives. Representative of this collection is a magnificent view of a clematis-covered bathhouse surrounded by peonies (pl. 9).

It was also during the first two decades of the century that the relationship between the du Pont country house at Winterthur and its surrounding landscape became firmly fixed in du Pont's mind. The need to integrate architecture with the adjacent landscape was no doubt reinforced for him when in 1914 he went to England with his father, Henry Algernon du Pont, to visit country homes and gardens there.

Soon after Henry Francis du Pont became master of Winterthur in 1926, he began planning a grand landscape garden that would complement his antiques collection and reflect his intention eventually to turn his house into a public museum. To this end, he called on family friend and noted landscape architect Marian Cruger Coffin. Although Coffin had been heavily influenced by classical design in graduate school at Massachusetts Institute of Technology, she reached an important turning point in the early 1900s when she traveled to England and met famous landscape architect Gertrude Jekyll. Coffin was tremendously impressed by the way Jekyll synthesized the "natural garden" concept and a more classical design approach. Much of Coffin's later work would reflect Jekyll's sensitivity to horticulture and her engaging use of color. The letters, drawings, and photographs in the Marian Coffin Collection reveal Coffin's pervasive influence on Winterthur from the 1930s until her death in 1957. Coffin's papers are also important in documenting her work for other notable clients, including Marshall Field, Frederick Frelinghuysen, Edward F. Hutton, William Marshall Bullitt, Childs Frick, and Frederick Vanderbilt,

Fig. 26. Robert Brost, bathhouse, 1935. Stereograph; H. 3½″, w. 7″.

When Henry Francis du Pont added a massive addition to his house at Winterthur in 1929/ 30, the upper terrace of the Formal Garden was altered dramatically. A large rectangular swimming pool replaced the original smaller pool, and two bathhouses supplanted the Pavilion. This stereo view taken in May 1935 shows one of the new bathhouses.

as well as in recording work for her own gardens at Wendover in Watch Hill, Rhode Island, and in New Haven, Connecticut.

With Coffin's help, Winterthur gardens had been spectacularly refined and enlarged by the late 1930s. In recognition of these improvements, in 1935 du Pont hired Robert Brost, an expert in stereoscopic photography, to make stereographic prints, some of them hand tinted, of key areas of the garden. The resulting stereo views, which are now in the Robert Brost Stereocard Collection, record a critical period in the development of Winterthur garden. A particularly lovely image shows one of the imposing bathhouses in the swimming pool area (fig. 26).

As Winterthur became a public museum and developed a graduate program in early American culture, the library began collecting publications on landscape gardening that would augment the fine body of horticultural literature amassed by Henry Algernon and Henry Francis du Pont. It also focused its collecting efforts on securing works that would provide a broad English and Continental background for American landscape theory and design in the nineteenth and twentieth centuries. As a result, Winterthur Library now lists among its holdings André Le Nôtre's untitled treatise on formal Continental gardening styles and John Laurence's *Clergy-Man's Recreation* on English vernacular gardening. Other eighteenth-century titles in the library focus on French and Italian formal garden design, as well as oriental gardening. Nineteenth-century publica-

Fig. 27. "An Aviary." From John Buonarotti Papworth, *Hints on Ornamental Gardening: Consisting of a Series of Designs for Garden Buildings, Useful and Decorative Gates, Fences, Railroads, &c.* (London: R. Ackermann, 1823), pl. 6. Page: H. 11″, W. 7½″.

In the nineteenth century, aviaries were typically designed to embellish extensive gardens, not for practical purposes. Papworth recommended that they "be situated on a small island in a retired portion of the estate, not far distant from the mansion" (p. 54).

Fig. 28. "Rhynlandsche Voetmaat." From G. Van Laar, *Magazijn van Tuin-Sieraaden* (Amsterdam: J. de Ruyter, [1802]), pl. 157. Page: H. 11¾″, W. 9″.

These images of a country inn and garden bridge create an atmosphere of safety and reflection, feelings often fostered by rural landscape literature.

tions in the library include Richard Morris's *Essays on Landscape Gardening and on Uniting Picturesque Effect with Rural Scenery*, Humphrey Repton's *Fragments on the Theory and Practice of Landscape Gardening*, and John B. Papworth's *Hints on Ornamental Gardening*. The last contains marvelous illustrations, one of them of an aviary amid a lush garden (fig. 27). Beautiful illustrations of landscapes are also found in G. Van Laar's *Magazijn van Tuin-Sieraaden* (fig. 28) and John Allen's *Victoria Regia* (fig. 29). In both England and America, the influence of formal or classical design in landscape gardening diminished as the influence of the rural aesthetic increased. Richard Morris suggested the importance of the rural aesthetic as early as 1825, a point reinforced by the title of John C. Loudon's 1842 treatise on the science and practice of landscape management, *The Suburban Horticulturalist*. After Loudon, many works such as the *Villa Gardener* focused squarely on the suburbs.

In addition to the above printed and archival works, the library has been fortunate in collecting a number of manuscript and personal items that help researchers to understand landscape gardening in America. An anonymous nineteenth-century scrapbook entitled "Waste Book" contains a rare landscape drawing of Fairhill, the eighteenth-century Philadelphia home of Isaac Norris. The library also has photographs of the garden of H. Gates Lloyd at Allgates in Haverford, Pennsylvania. But the most engaging item in the collection might well be the keepsake album of Mary Eliza Bachman, dated 1835. This little book contains watercolor drawings of flowers and birds and a frontispiece illustration of a woman contem-

Fig. 29. Water lily. From John Allen, *Victoria Regia; or, The Great Water Lily of America* (Boston: Dutton and Wentworth, 1854), pl. [6]. Page: H. 22″, W. 29″.

Discovered in South America in 1803, the water lily was given the name Victoria Regia in 1837.

plating her garden. Bachman has also pressed a dried flower into a page and recorded her spontaneous thoughts on gardens and nature, including a poem entitled "Reflections on a Flower Plant Destroyed by Frost."

The poem below the frontispiece of Bachman's keepsake album rings true for landscape lovers of all times and ages, including Henry Francis du Pont: "Gay pleasure-grounds are my delight / Adorned with flowers select & bright."

Art and Artists

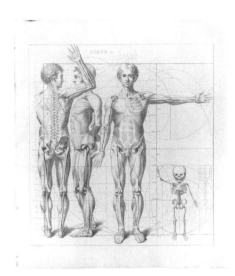

Fig. 30. Human figures. From John Rubens Smith, *A Compendium of Picturesque Anatomy Applied to the Arts* (Boston: By the author, 1827), pl. 1. Page: H. 18⅜″, W. 16″.

The irascible artist Smith published several instructional books as he moved his drawing academy from Boston to Brooklyn to Philadelphia. While in Boston he published his *Compendium*, a handsome anatomy publication for artists. Letters of "approbation" from Washington Allston and Gilbert Stuart were placed prominently on the title page.

Pictures are an integral part of our everyday world. A newspaper or magazine without pictures is impossible to imagine. In the eighteenth century, people also enjoyed pictures in magazines and almanacs, or on shop signs and trade cards. The library's hand-colored trade card for Raphaelle and Rembrandt Peale demonstrates only one of the many uses to which illustrations have been put. By the end of the nineteenth century, illustrated books, magazines, greeting cards, calendars, and sheet music were found in many American homes, while illustrated product labels, billheads, and letterheads enlivened the business world. In addition, most American cities boasted at least one commercial art gallery where framed paintings could be purchased.

Among both professional artists and amateurs, a lively market developed in America and Europe for instructional manuals and books on aesthetics, perspective, color theory, physiognomy, and anatomy. John Rubens Smith's *Compendium of Picturesque Anatomy*, for example, was specifically designed to aid artists in drawing human figures (fig. 30). Another manual concerned with the human figure is Cipriani and Bartolozzi's *Rudiments of Drawing*, which begins with simple drawing lessons—studies of eyes, mouths, ears, hands, and feet—and proceeds to more complicated views of posed figures, draped and undraped, or classical sculpture. Apparently, authors of instructional manuals generally subscribed to the confident declaration on the cover of John Gadsby Chapman's *American Drawing Book*: "Anyone who can learn to write, can learn to draw." Persons aspiring to gentility were further encouraged to draw by authors such as Henry Peacham, a seventeenth-century version of Miss Manners, who in the *Compleat Gentleman* considered the ability to draw "a quality most commendable."

Some instructional manuals covered a variety of techniques, among them Thomas E. B. Shillinglaw's handwritten instructional volume, which promised lessons in, for example, drawing; oil, watercolor, and velvet painting; oriental and mezzo tinting; crayoning; and transferring. Others, however, were earmarked for young men or women, either as a means to greater gentility or as a training tool for draftsmen. Draftsmen were fortunate in being able to select titles to suit specific occupational needs. *Vari-*

ous *Sketches of Shipping* and *Introduction to Drawing Ships* were intended for draftsmen in shipbuilding, while Seth Eastman's *Treatise on Topographical Drawing* provided military cadets with detailed instructions for drawing maps that would facilitate the movement of cavalry, artillery, and infantry. For sketching or needlework, young draftsmen's sisters could select designs from portfolios of flower prints such as Kilburn and Dodd's *New Book of Sprigs of Flowers*. Also available was George Brookshaw's illustrated volume on sketching bouquets, a work that included suggestions on the best way to arrange flowers and the most appropriate colors for arrangements. Young ladies with particularly nimble fingers could copy the lively and sometimes amusing silhouettes in Barbara Anne Townshend's *Introduction to the Art of Cutting Groups of Figures, Flowers, Birds, etc. in Black Paper* (fig. 31). Perhaps the most intriguing teaching device owned by the library, though, is *The Protean Figure and Metamorphic Costumes* published in 1811 (figs. 32, 33). Usually described as a paper doll, the Protean figure was actually meant to be used as an artistic model. The customer who purchased this male paper figure would dress it in costume and place it against a colored aquatint landscape that served as a neutral backdrop. The publishers of the *Protean Figure*, S. and J. Fuller, were known for producing handsome drawing manuals, such as David Cox's *Treatise on Landscape Painting* and *Young Artist's Companion*.

In the early nineteenth century, the rage for watercolor landscape painting fueled the market for an extraordinary body of hand-colored instructional books. John Laporte's *Progress of a Water-colored Drawing* demonstrates the development of a single drawing through fourteen stages, beginning with soft-ground etching and adding layers of watercolor washes until the drawing is completed. Equally magnificent is John

Fig. 31. Cutting figures. From Barbara Anne Townshend, *Introduction to the Art of Cutting Groups of Flowers, Figures, Birds, etc. in Black Paper* (London: Edward Orme, 1815–16), pl. 1. Page: H. 12½", W. 18".

Townshend advised those wishing to learn paper cutting to "form the figures with the scissors without the aid of a pencil," beginning with the feet and back and then proceeding to the hands. Edward Orme, the book's publisher, is best known for producing *Gilpin's Day*, a fine landscape drawing manual with watercolored aquatint illustrations.

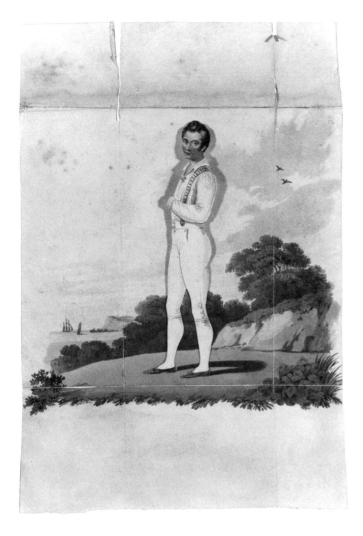

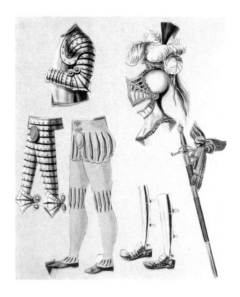

Fig. 33. Knight's costume for the Protean figure in figure 32. From *The Protean Figure and Metamorphic Costumes* (London: S. and J. Fuller, 1811).

In addition to the complete set of armor seen here, the Protean figure came with twelve hand-colored sets of clothes, including a naval uniform, a walking outfit, and a Turkish costume.

Fig. 32. Protean figure. From *The Protean Figure and Metamorphic Costumes* (London: S. and J. Fuller, 1811). Page: H. 15¾″, W. 10¼″.

Purchasers of the Protean figure were to place the figure on the colored aquatint landscape so that his "Heels fill up space left for them in the shaded parts of the gravel walk."

Hassell's *Aqua Pictura*, which illustrates each of the steps—etching the outline, applying monochrome aquatint ground, filling in light and shaded areas, and applying transparent watercolor washes—required to produce the work's sixteen aquatints modeled on the work of the best contemporary watercolor landscapists. In addition, Hassell's text is interspersed with dabs of actual watercolors to show the exact tint of the colors described in the text.

Another important source of information about artists and their work is the pocket-size notebooks that many artists kept for spontaneously sketching people, events, or scenery; recording recipes for mixing paint; and penning observations about the work of other artists. John Lewis Krimmel's seven sketchbooks are particularly illuminating for their

little `head . However v
needut have been afraid
there is only Miss Hosmer
the american sculptress
&c .

Good humoured with short
hair &
pellicoals &
neatest little
boots

Fig. 34. Sketch of Harriet Hosmer. From Anna Thackery to Mary James, Warsash, Titchfield, Eng., September 23, 1867. Page: H. 7″, W. 4½″.

Hosmer defied convention by becoming a professional sculptress and establishing a studio in Rome where she created full-size figures in marble on classical and literary subjects. Despite her rather eccentric manner of dressing, she was well liked among Rome's expatriate society and traveled widely visiting friends throughout Europe.

detailed watercolor depictions of American domestic life in the 1810s and 1820s. By contrast, John La Farge's sketchbook is less a record of his surroundings than his mental notebook, a medium for recording stages in the process of creation.

Much insight into the private impressions that inform an artist's work can be gained through studying his or her correspondence. The library's collection of long, chatty letters that painter Thomas Sully and his daughter Blanche wrote home to Philadelphia during an 1837/38 trip to London describe meetings with various artists, dining out, and art exhibitions, as well as provide valuable information about the progress of Sully's portrait of young Queen Victoria. Frederic Edwin Church's letters to his parents and sister Charlotte while traveling in South America in 1853 describe a more exotic adventure than Sully's. Descriptions of artists in the correspondence of their contemporaries can be equally illuminating about an artist's work or character. While visiting friends in England, Harriet Hosmer, an American sculptress who received a £100,000 commission for a memorial to Lincoln, was briefly but insightfully described in a letter by another houseguest, Anna Thackery: "Miss Hosmer . . . is very funny & good humoured with short hair & petticoats & neatest little boots & so like a merry little   that its impossible not to like her." The description is accompanied by a sketch of the sculptress (fig. 34).

What pictures did Americans actually hang on their walls? The answer is often elusive, but sources such as the inventory left by Thomas Gilpin, a Wilmington, Delaware, paper manufacturer, provide a glimpse inside American homes. Compiled between 1839 and 1844, the inventory is unusual in listing the paintings and prints in Gilpin's collection by both their titles and their artist's name. Gilpin's taste and pocketbook led him to collect the work of European old masters as well as that of contemporary American artists. In addition to paintings of biblical scenes by Claude Lorrain, he owned two landscapes by Thomas Doughty, a framed drawing by Benjamin Latrobe, and several drawings by John James Barralet, as well as numerous engravings.

Household inventories of home libraries are also useful sources of information about the public's taste in art. Gilpin's library contained numerous works on art and aesthetics, an appropriate assemblage for a gentleman collector. Gilpin's inventory reveals that he owned Charles Joseph Hullmandel's *Art of Drawing on Stone* and Laporte's *Progress of a Water-colored Drawing* among other works. The library of New York lithographer George Endicott was more utilitarian, reflecting a working artist's need for sources of visual ideas. Listed in the inventory of his estate were "Le Brun's *Passions*" and "Knights books." The former probably refers to a reprint of Charles Le Brun's seventeenth-century study of physiognomy, while the latter refers to the highly popular publications of Frederick Knight who issued countless books illustrating ornamental motifs for artists during the 1820s and 1830s. Both Le Brun's and Knight's books were compendiums of useful images and motifs for artists, somewhat akin to pattern books produced for craftsmen. Such evidence about the kinds of art books owned by patrons and artists significantly enlivens our understanding of the American art scene.

Documents at Winterthur about everyday life in America allow researchers to understand better the lives of both professional and amateur artists. The great number of publications addressed to amateurs attests to the public's hunger for artistic expression. As Americans increasingly took up the brush or the needle as a leisure activity, they also became more receptive to works by professional artists and increasingly welcomed into the home paintings and sculpture as decorative items. The public was also exposed to art in the form of advertisements, and the library supplies ample materials for studying the important role that pictures played in commerce. Winterthur Library's collections concerning professional, amateur, and commercial art provide a comprehensive description of the artistic efforts of Americans and demonstrate the contribution of many kinds of artists to American culture.

Childhood

Fig. 35. Paper doll and accessories. From *La Psyché; ou, Le petit magasin de modes* (France, 1820–29). Page: H. 4".

Psyché refers to the free-standing mirror, a new furniture form introduced in the early nineteenth century and to the beautiful mortal with whom Cupid fell in love.

It is astonishing that any paper dolls, games, and books created for children survived their loving but vigorous hands. Modern historians owe an enormous debt to adult collectors of such seemingly frivolous items. One such collector, Maxine Waldron, donated her fine collection of children's books and paper toys to Winterthur Library in 1974. Containing materials from the early 1600s to the 1960s, the Maxine Waldron Collection of Children's and Paper Toys reflects changing attitudes toward childhood over four centuries.

The most fragile items in the collection are paper dolls, of which Waldron was especially fond. As an only child who often had to play alone, Waldron spent many happy hours with her paper dolls, a fact reflected in the hundreds of paper dolls in her collection. Among the rarest items in the Waldron Collection is a chenille-embroidery-on-silk costume of a seventeenth-century paper doll. Such dolls were actually used by dressmakers to illustrate the latest fashions for wealthy ladies rather than as toys for children. A similar purpose was served by the faceless figures in a tiny volume of watercolors titled *Coiffures*. Illustrating elaborate French coiffures and gowns, these figures are intended to be placed over a head shown in an accompanying oval frame. The above rare fashion dolls seem plain, however, when compared with *La psyché*, an early nineteenth-century paper doll with elaborate costumes that include hats, a shawl, and a cloak, as well as a tiny full-length mirror (fig. 35).

Advances in printing and coloring in the mid nineteenth century enabled children to choose from an enormous variety of printed dolls for the first time. The first lithographed American paper doll, *Fanny Gray*, appeared in Boston in 1854. Fanny came with five action costumes, a bonnet, a stand, a paper background, and a booklet. Soon paper-doll families were widely available, and personalities such as Jenny Lind, Fanny Elssler, Tom Thumb, Napoleon, and Queen Victoria became favorite playthings. Boys also enjoyed paper dolls, playing with paper soldiers and military heroes. When printed dolls were unavailable, children often made their own from paper and bits of fabric in their mother's scrap bag. Anson Davies Fitz Randolph's *Paper Dolls and How to Make Them* and C. D. Allair's *Paper Doll's Furniture: How to Make It* are two books in the 1850s that provided children with ideas and guidelines for making dolls themselves. The library owns several sets of handmade paper dolls.

The Waldron Collection also includes numerous settings and accessories for dolls. *The Dairy and the Poultry Yard* contains forty-two paper barnyard animals on wooden stands that can be set against a paper background, while the *L'intérieur de la poupée*, which comes with a paper-doll family and furniture, including a fabric rug, is a three-sided doll parlor. Another paper toy collected by Waldron is a late nineteenth-century puppet house by Lothar Meggendorfer. Among the most elaborate three-dimensional toys in the collection is *The Forty Thieves: A Drama*, a toy theater that has paper-doll characters, scenery, and a play script. Waldron was also fascinated by paper toys unconnected with dolls, such as card games, panoramas, puzzles, and peep shows. The last are accordion-folded tunnels through which one peeks to see a tableau or an imaginary setting.

Fortunately, researchers attempting to understand the experience of childhood in earlier ages are not dependent on surviving toys alone. The business records and advertisements of manufacturers and distributors provide much useful information about playthings and other aspects of daily life. From sources such as Lewis Page's business correspondence, students of childhood now know that many toys in America in the early nineteenth century were made in Germany. According to his letters, Page, a New York merchant, imported German toys between 1829 and 1833. Another source of information on toys is an extraordinary illustrated catalogue of German toys, dating from 1818 to 1839. This catalogue, which consists of 135 watercolors by an unknown distributor, provides a rich resource for studying United States toy imports in the early nineteenth century and the influence of German prototypes on American manufacturers (pl. 10).

Since Waldron was as fond of children's books as she was of children's toys, she also had a strong collection of written works for children. Among the most appealing are those with "pop-up" and movable parts. Before the term *pop-up* was coined in the 1930s, publishers used other words for these attention-getting devices. German publisher Ernest Nister called some of his inventive movable books "panoramas" and referred to others as "transformations" or "revolving pictures." Transformations are small picture books with illustrations on flaps that, when turned, transform one image into another. Whatever they have been called at various times, such works take into account children's interest in movable objects and short attention spans.

Waldron's interest in books was not limited to those with clever de-

Fig. 36. "Fanny in a red cloak, with a hat in her hand, begging her bread." From *The History of Little Fanny* (2d ed.; Philadelphia: Morgan and Yeager, 1825), pl. 3. Page: H. 4½″, w. 3½″.

"Can this be Fanny, once so neat and clean?" According to the story, Fanny was too fond of playing and not interested in being an obedient child. "But learn from this," admonished the narrator. Fanny was kidnapped from her well-to-do family by beggars when she strayed to admire a shop window (p. 7).

vices. She also collected books intended to teach children lessons about life and the world around them. The woodcuts of a seventeenth-century work by Johann Amos Comenius entitled *Orbis Sensualium Pictus* comprise a visual encyclopedia of "all the chief things that are in the world and man's employments therein" (1777 London ed., title p.). The continued popularity of such visual compendiums is attested by *A Museum and Panorama for Instruction and Amusement of Our Young Friends*, which features exquisite hand-colored engravings of exotic birds, plants, and animals, and Ann Taylor Gilbert's *City Scenes; or, A Peep into London*, which intersperses views of the city's monuments and other sights with lessons about good and bad occupations. An American version is the American Sunday-School Union's *City Sights for Country Eyes*, which depicts oystermen, icemen, ragmen, and others at work.

Commonly, books that introduced children to work as well as more familiar storybooks contained instruction on good behavior. The cautionary tale of Little Fanny, originally published in London in 1810, depicts a vain and idle young lady who is rescued from a series of misadventures that would have undoubtedly resulted in moral and social disgrace. The success of this work inspired both reproductions and imitations. Its illustrations were reproduced in *Die Kleine Fanny*, published circa 1815, and served as a model for *Phébé; ou, La Piété Filiale* in 1817. One of the nicest editions of this moralistic tale is a hand-colored Philadelphia version titled *The History of Little Fanny* (fig. 36). In the book's happy ending, Fanny becomes "Pious, modest, diligent and mild, belov'd by all, a good and happy child" (p. 15) (fig. 37). *The History of Little Goody Twoshoes, Little Helen; or, A Day in the Life of a Naughty Girl*, Arnaud Berquin's *Blossoms of Morality*, and Alice Bradley Haven's "*All's Not Gold That Glitters*," also made little attempt to disguise their pedagogic purpose. Neither did the board game entitled *Newton's New Game of Virtue Rewarded and Vice Punished for the Amusement of Youth of Both Sexes*.

In addition to providing social historians with information about the social and moral conduct expected of children, storybooks convey information about children's activities and desires difficult to discover from other sources. The woodcuts of *A Little Pretty Pocket-Book* show boys playing hopscotch and a handball game popularly known in England as "game of fives" (fig. 38). The activities for girls depicted in *Minnie's Playroom; or, How to Practice Calisthenics* were equally strenuous, rivaling present-day aerobics. And although Lilla Elizabeth Kelley's *Three Hundred Things a Bright Girl Can Do* has instructions on such traditional activities as rugmaking, needlework, and paper-flower making, it also contains lessons in wood carving, taxidermy, and the law. Such publica-

Fig. 37. "Fanny restored to her former station." From *The History of Little Fanny* (2d ed.; Philadelphia: Morgan and Yeager, 1825), pl. 7. Page: H. 4½″, W. 3½″.

Fanny became an errand girl for a fish monger and then for a dairyman. One day she found herself sent to her mother's house to deliver butter. "Alas! I cannot enter there," she cried, but happily her mother welcomed her home. This last illustration in the story shows the restored Fanny, "no longer idle, proud, or vain" (p. 15).

Fig. 38. "Fives." From *A Little Pretty Pocket-Book, Intended for the Instruction and Amusement of Little Master Tommy and Pretty Miss Polly* (Worcester, Mass.: Isaiah Thomas, 1787), p. 46. Page: H. 1⅛″, W. 1⅝″.

Four boys are shown here playing fives, a game in which the players alternately hit a ball against a wall with their hands instead of a racket.

tions are more reliable sources of information about how children actually spent their leisure time than works such as *Little Fanny*, which project an adult view of idealized children.

What did children actually think of the toys, books, and games that scholars study as clues to the lives of children in earlier ages? Possibly such artifacts survive because they were the most widely available. On the other hand, they may have survived because they were so unpopular and, consequently, so unused that they remained in the bottom of a toy box or the top of a shelf. Such conundrums will continue to absorb researchers who must consider all kinds of materials to appreciate fully how childhood was experienced.

Courtesy and Etiquette

In the ordinary course of daily life, few people think of stopping to consult an etiquette book on any but the most ceremonial of occasions, but arbiters of personal behavior have dispensed advice at least since written literature first appeared. Over the centuries, such compendia evolved and mutated into the etiquette books of today. While such manuals are prescriptive rather than descriptive, they offer enough clues to contemporary behavior to constitute a rich source of information about the rituals and routines of everyday life in the past and of the values and standards they reflect.

Courtesy books are the immediate predecessors of etiquette books of the last 150 years. Through the end of the eighteenth century, courtesy books codified the qualities and standards gentlemen and gentlewomen should possess and inculcated these standards by applying them to tasks and situations in daily life. Few genres contain less truly original thought, and few cannibalize each other more over the centuries. Generally, courtesy books summarized already accepted rules of behavior that had originated at court or at the great houses of the nobility. While most such books, especially those written for women, pay dutiful attention to Christian virtues, some cynical authors—most famously Machiavelli and Lord Chesterfield—stressed the appearance rather than the attainment of virtue. One work of this ilk in Winterthur Library is Baltazar Gracian y Morales's *Courtiers Manual Oracle*, a 1685 London translation of a Spanish original, which proffers such advice as finding out "the weak side of every one."

In the early nineteenth century, the appearance of newly monied middle classes sprung from obscure backgrounds led to the replacement of the courtesy book by the manual of "etiquette," a word first used in its modern sense, appropriately enough, in a 1750 letter of Lord Chesterfield's. Unlike courtesy books, etiquette manuals aimed at quick results. Since authors of such treatises could not assume that their readers had genteel backgrounds—indeed, they quite often came from the lower social orders—etiquette authors became increasingly dictatorial in their directives, often emphasizing their authority and social standing by signing their works with real or bogus titles and descriptions. Unsurprisingly, rules

Fig. 39. "Walking and saluting passing by." From F. Nivelon, *The Rudiments of Genteel Behavior* ([London?], 1737), pl. 2. Page: H. 11″, W. 8½″.

Nivelon's manual assumes that for both men and women, body language is as eloquent as speech. For those wishing to appear truly genteel, Nivelon rigidly prescribes and illustrates correct methods for standing, walking, and dancing.

for the minutiae of outward behavior characterize the etiquette book of the nineteenth century.

The library's extensive holdings of courtesy and etiquette publications include copies of the most popular seventeenth-century English courtesy books, works known to have been owned in this country, even though little scope could have been afforded to much of their advice. Few men in the colonies would have had the time to attain such gentlemanly accomplishments recommended by Henry Peacham in the *Compleat Gentleman* as "Painting and drawing in Oyl" and hawking. Like those for men, English courtesy books written for women, such as Richard Allestree's *Ladies Calling* and William Kenrick's *Whole Duty of a Woman*, were popular here. A particularly appealing courtesy book for women is Richard Brathwaite's *English Gentlewoman*. In a chapter entitled "Reproof Touching Apparell," Brathwaite cautions his readers to avoid "Sumptuousnesse, Softnesse, Strangenesse, and Superfluousnesse," adding that "Gentility is not known by what we weare, but what we are," a sentiment echoed by many advice books ever since. Most courtesy books for women, like Brathwaite's, emphasized modesty, meekness, and Christian virtues as the most desirable female qualities. An unusual courtesy book for the period was Sir John Barnard's *Present for an Apprentice* (1642), a practical compendium of advice for aspiring merchants that was so realistic in its approach to mercantile success that it was reprinted in Philadelphia as late as 1774.

Striking visual evidence of high eighteenth-century manners appears in F. Nivelon's handsome *Rudiments of Genteel Behavior*, which illustrates the correct posture for walking, dancing, and greeting others (fig. 39). Nivelon's advice is echoed in a Boston publication called *A Guide to Politeness* by dancing master Francis D. Nichols, whose charming illustrations of ballroom manners recall those of the earlier volume (fig. 40).

An important and enduring strain of advice literature took the form of counsel from a real or putative parent to his or her children. An example in Winterthur's collection is Isaac Taylor's *Advice to the Teens*, Taylor surely being among the first to use the word *teens*. The library's copies of two similar works, John Gregory's *Father's Legacy to His Daughters* and Mrs. Peddle's *Rudiments of Taste . . . from a Mother to Her Daughters*, both reprinted in Chambersburg, Pennsylvania, in the late eighteenth century, have been bound together by a later owner with a sense of humor. Bound with them is a late nineteenth-century advertising pamphlet for the popular theatrical pot-boiler *Only a Farmer's Daughter*.

The problem of defining a truly American etiquette, an issue raised

Fig. 40. "Come, and trip it as you go, On the light fantastic toe." From Francis D. Nichols, *A Guide to Politeness; or, A System of Directions for the Acquirement of Ease, Propriety, and Elegance of Manners . . .* (Boston: Lincoln and Edmands, 1810), frontispiece. Page: H. 6¾", w. 4".

The charming illustrations in this volume on ballroom etiquette by an "Instructor of dancing in Boston" reflect the demise of Puritan influence on social customs by 1810.

'Come, and trip it as you go: On the light fantastic toe."

early in the nineteenth century, produced such works as expurgated and Americanized versions of Lord Chesterfield; E. Cooley's manual of the etiquette observed in Washington, our national court; and Charles Butler's *American Lady* and *American Gentleman* in 1836. Butler's epitome of gentility was, not surprisingly, George Washington. However, reprints of popular English titles continued to appear, such as the charming *Mirror of the Graces*, which contains the first colored fashion plates found in an American publication, and Edward Caswall's amusing *Sketches of Young Ladies and Young Gentlemen*, which pokes fun at ill behavior in both its text and its illustrations. Such humor, however, was rare in the nineteenth century, for readers of etiquette manuals were entering an age of anxiety, although writers of these works were entering an age of opportunity. For their financially comfortable but socially untutored audience, publishers issued such titles as the Countess of Calabrella's *Ladies' Science of Etiquette* and Samuel R. Wells's *How to Behave*, both inexpensive publications aimed at a mass audience. Toward the end of the century, Florence Marion Hall's *Correct Thing in Good Society* simply tabulated dos and don'ts on facing pages. According to Hall, it is correct to use a colored cloth for luncheon tables; it is not correct to use such a cloth for dinner. An 1891 publication by "Censor" titled *Don't* simplified etiquette by listing only behaviors to avoid. Some of Censor's advice is quite sensible. Censor's recommendations not to use endearments insincerely or to borrow books without returning them are as valuable today as they were when first penned. However, the caution against wearing diamonds in the daytime is less applicable to readers now than it was for the audience for whom it was written.

Although the rules set forth in the courtesy and etiquette manuals of earlier ages at times appear impossibly complex to modern, more relaxed audiences, some advice still holds. Today's readers would do well to remember Wells's counsel that although the forms for expressing politeness vary with time and place, politeness itself "is always the same."

NEVILLE THOMPSON

Pleasure and Ceremony

Paradoxically, the very process of studying past lives can distance researchers from them by reducing their complex texture to bald, cheerless facts about long working hours, primitive household chores, and incessant toil. However, a large body of evidence suggests that people have always found ways to enjoy themselves and to mark important events in their lives with formal and often moving ceremonies and rituals.

People of the past played amateur sports and attended professional matches. They hunted and fished. They danced, made music themselves, and listened with enjoyment to the music of others. They traveled and brought back from those travels an amazing range of souvenirs, from papier-mâché boxes to the Elgin marbles. They painted, embroidered, and made fancywork for bazaars. At home in the evenings, families played charades, chess, and paper games and told stories. They kept scrapbooks, wrote poetry, tended pets, and planted indoor gardens. They joined societies of all kinds and founded others, and in the nineteenth century, as the leisured middle class grew, they did all these things with even greater fervor. In large and small groups, they performed memorable rituals ranging from the solemn to the ridiculous, which they then chronicled in letters, diaries, magazine articles, how-to-do-it books, sketches, postcards, and stereopticon views. Winterthur Library is rich in this evidence, so rich that only a small sampling can be included here.

Certainly one of the grandest of the library's volumes commemorating a special occasion is Thomas Jean Pichon's *Sacre et couronnement de Louis XVI*, a fete book recording the costumes and ceremonies prescribed for the ill-fated king's coronation at Reims. In its luxurious binding, handsome printing, fine paper, and splendid illustrations, the book is precisely evocative of its era and totally unaware of its approaching and violent end. More democratic rites, although in an equally splendid setting, were performed in the New Masonic Temple of Philadelphia, dedicated in 1875. The volume issued by the lodge's library committee for the occasion is unusual for its tipped-in illustrations, which are photographs of the building's exotic interiors and imposing exterior. An even earlier photographically illustrated book was issued by Charles J. Stillé as a catalogue of the Great Central Sanitary Fair in Philadelphia in 1864, a bazaar staged

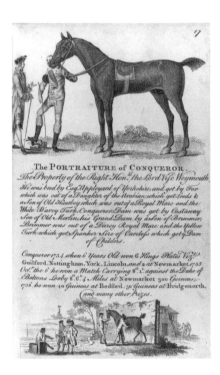

Fig. 41. "The Portraiture of Conqueror." From James Roberts, *The Sportsman's Pocket Companion* ([London: Henry Roberts, 1760?]), leaf 17. Page: H. 8⅝″, W. 5½″.

An eighteenth-century *Who's Who* of notable racehorses, and not, incidentally, of their titled owners, this handsome volume is engraved throughout. At the foot of each page, the engraver has added engaging vignettes of the horse's everyday life.

to benefit the Union forces. The book's photographs reveal the great scale of the fair and, more intimately, the massive and elaborate silver Union Vase contributed by Philadelphia jewelers Bailey and Company for the occasion. Equally splendid are the color illustrations of the religious ceremonies of the Mandan Indians recorded by George Catlin, an explorer and painter of the native Americans of the West. Another of the library's impressive volumes concerning grand ceremonies is George D. Carroll's *Art of Dinner Giving*. A disguised trade catalogue for Dempsey and Carroll, a stationery firm that catered to high society, the volume reverently furnishes, in minute detail, guest lists, menus, and table decorations for some of the most excessive entertainments of the Gilded Age, including banquets for General Grant and the "elegant Private Dinner" staged by Mrs. D. H. McAlpin of Fifth Avenue to welcome Cleopatra's Needle to New York City. At McAlpin's party, the menus folded into hieroglyph-covered obelisks. The selection of foods served at the party, however, is disappointingly unimaginative, considering the opportunity. Only "Punch Cleopatra" suggests an Egyptian touch.

On less spectacular occasions than those described above, Americans sought pleasure and amusement from various sources. Both in public and in private, music and dance have always been sources of pleasure. A rare early Philadelphia imprint edited by John Aitken called the *Scots Musical Museum* is a collection of folk songs for home musicians, such as the young lady playing a pianoforte in the advertising broadside of piano-maker George E. Blake. As early as 1817, a French "Professor of Dancing" in Philadelphia named J. H. Gourdoux-Doux published his *Elements and Principles of the Art of Dancing*, a forerunner of many guides to the increasingly complex etiquette and dance figures of the day. Later in the century, as balls became more elaborate, fancy dress parties were the rage. A manual by Ardern Holt illustrates hundreds of costumes for the unimaginative, ranging from the "Hornet" to Mary, queen of Scots. Nightlife of a riskier sort is described in *Hints to Men about Town* by "a Sporting Surgeon," a guide for Regency dandies to London's seamy side. By day, English gentlemen cherished racehorses, as James Roberts's beautifully engraved *Sportsman's Pocket Companion* of 1760 testifies (fig. 41).

Women, meanwhile, had amusements of a safer nature. Needlework and all sorts of crafts proliferated, as surviving manuals of handicraft attest. Forgotten skills—skeletonizing leaves, painting on velvet, and making hair jewelry—all had their practitioners, and many women compiled their handiwork in scrapbooks and albums. Scrapbooks in the library's collections contain, among other things, greeting cards, fabric swatches, and an entire imaginary house interior assembled from paper ephemera.

Fig. 42. "The Swing." From Mlle. St.-Sernin, *Healthful Sports for Young Ladies* (London: R. Ackermann, [1822]), facing p. 1. Page: H. 5″, W. 7¾″.

This picture book is typical of the appealing early nineteenth-century color-plate publications issued by Rudolph Ackermann. The young ladies' sport seems to be more picturesque than strenuous.

Fig. 43. "Coasting Backwards—Sitting Side-Saddle on Top Stay." From Isabel Marks, *Fancy Cycling for Amateurs* (London: Sands, 1901), p. 33. Page: H. 7½″, W. 5⅜″.

Bicycling became a craze during the later years of the nineteenth century. As this illustration demonstrates, daredevils were not content with simply remaining upright and in motion.

As Mlle. St.-Sernin's *Healthful Sports for Young Ladies* records, women in the early nineteenth century took up outdoor sports with great zeal (fig. 42). The anonymous *Archer's Guide*, R. Fellow's *Game of Croquet*, and Isabel Marks's *Fancy Cycling* (fig. 43) all taught sports that women as well as men could enjoy, and a member of a famous New England sporting-goods manufacturing firm, Mary Orvis Marbury, compiled a sumptuously illustrated volume about fly-fishing, *Favorite Flies and Their Histories* (pl. 11).

Family amusements included card games, charades, and board games, some of which—namely, Parcheesi, Authors, and Jackstraws—appeared in the 1872 Milton Bradley Company catalogue. Together, families looked at the world through that photographic wonder, the stereopticon, as the library's instrument and slides attest. Other family-centered amusements, such as those celebrating traditional American holidays, are reflected in the library's delightful profusion of nineteenth-century greeting cards in the Thelma Seeds Mendsen Collection, which depict everything from St. Patrick's Day elves to tonsured Santa Clauses in monks' robes. In the second half of the nineteenth century especially, Americans amused themselves by collecting nature specimens such as birds' eggs, pressed flowers, ferns, and mushrooms. *Leaf and Flower Pictures and How to Make Them* is just one of many works on the subject of collecting and working natural objects to decorate the home. The very well off, however, such as art collector W. H. Aspinwall whose painting galleries are described in a privately printed guide presented to H. F. du Pont's father, were as likely to collect art for enjoyment as to amass natural wonders.

Fig. 44. "The Egyptian." From James W. Tufts [Company], *Descriptive Catalogue of James W. Tufts' Arctic Soda-water Apparatus* (Boston, 1876), pl. facing p. 46. Page: H. 9⅝″, w. 6⁷/₁₆″.

Even utilitarian machinery wore historic clothing in the nineteenth century, and since the soda fountain had no specific historic precedent, it was free to be designed in any style that appealed to its manufacturer. Some examples in the Tufts catalogue are Gothic, while others remain uniquely his own.

Design Patented January 27, 1874.

THE EGYPTIAN.

Description and Prices on page 51.

Yet other entertainments, such as parades, circuses, and fireworks, were enjoyed by the public en masse. Amedée François Frezier's *Traité des jeux d'artifice* published in 1747 testifies to the long popularity of fireworks, just as Adam Forepaugh's *Catalogue of Living Wonders* does to the perennial appeal of the circus. Forepaugh's show, which featured "300 animals and birds" and "345 men and horses," must have made a brief sensation when it hit town. A more routinely accessible marvel of pleasure was soda fountains, which often received exotic treatments in the nineteenth century. Notable examples appear in an illustrated catalogue of the James W. Tufts company of Boston (fig. 44).

The volumes mentioned above reflect only a few of the many formal and informal pleasures of the past described in the library's collections. But all testify eloquently to the energy, curiosity, and self-reliance with which Americans pursued enjoyment and through which they recorded special occasions for posterity.

Cookbooks and Manuals of Domestic Economy

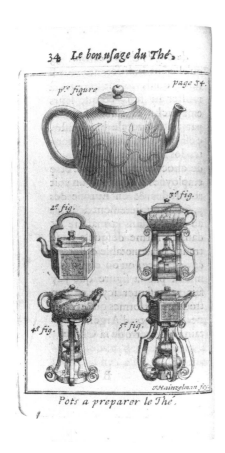

Fig. 45. "Pots a preparer le Thé." From Nicolas de Blegny, *Le bon usage du thé, du caffé et du chocolat pour la préservation et pour la guérison des maladies* (Lyon: Thomas Amaulry, 1687), p. 34. Page: H. 5⅞″, W. 3⅛″.

Coffee, tea, and chocolate were novelties when Blegny's book appeared. Blegny attempted to reassure drinkers about the beverages' medicinal values, instruct cooks in methods of brewing these drinks, and inform housewives about the correct implements and utensils for service, as in the teapots illustrated in this plate.

Cookbooks speak a universal language. Few subjects are as immediately accessible as food—our own, or other people's—and through the years many of us have amassed recipes ranging from the tried-and-true to extravagant pipe dreams. There have always been such assemblages. In Winterthur's collections we find, for instance, the manuscript cookbook of Hannah Huthwaite (1712) and E. Smith's *Compleat Housewife* (1742), the first cookbook published in America. Winterthur's copy of *The Compleat Housewife* is especially appealing since it is inscribed and dated by Jane Williams, its first owner, who purchased it in Williamsburg in 1743. The first printed cookbooks in both Europe and America record the food of the very well-to-do, although some recipes in these works reappear in various forms for centuries. A related genre is the receipt book, used both in the home and in the workplace. Predecessors of the domestic encyclopedia, receipt books contain recipes for cooking as well as for household products such as medicines, shellacs, and pesticides. Cookbooks and manuals of domestic economy provide valuable information about members of various classes in the seventeenth and eighteenth centuries, their values and preoccupations. Nicholas Blegny's *Bon usage du thé* (1687), for example, reveals fashionable society's fondness for the new drinks of coffee, tea, and chocolate and its interest in health by mingling remarks on methods for preparing the beverages with commentary on their medicinal value (fig. 45). Aimed at a similarly elegant section of society, Hannah Robertson's *Young Ladies School of Arts* indicates the interest of genteel housewives in the processes of shellworking and japanning, the concoction of cosmetics and jams, and the breeding of canary birds. Gervase Markham's *Countrey Contentments* and Madame Johnson's "instructions for young women," on the other hand, are more explicit about the hardships of housewifery. According to Markham, among the daunting responsibilities allotted to housewives are cooking, physic, surgery, brewing, baking, and spinning. Johnson, whose budget for a family in the "middling station in life" provides five pounds for lying-in "once in every two years," describes certain aspects of cooking in a no-nonsense style appropriate for such hard labor: "Dismember that heron . . . String that lamprey . . . splat that pike." Whatever one's station in the seventeenth and eighteenth centuries, cookbooks and receipt books reveal that meals were generally monotonous. Although Charles Carter's *Complete Practical Cook* announces that Carter was "lately cook to his Grace the Duke of Argyll," Carter's recipe for "cucumbers fryed" and his enthusiasm for "the boiling part" of cookery hardly make his cuisine appealing today. As the bills of fare and methods of preservation in *The Lady's Companion* indicate, English and colonial American diets were characterized by a preponderance of meat and baked goods, despite such tempting offerings as gilliflower wine. Another century would elapse before fruit and vegetables began to assume their present importance, encouraged by developments in commercial distribution and preservation technology.

The profound social and technological changes that occurred during the nineteenth century are mirrored in the increasing number of cookbooks and manuals of domestic economy that appeared then. Urbanization broke up rural extended households and placed many inexperienced wives in cities without mentors other than books. Technology not only made possible altered ways of arranging households and carrying out tasks but also fostered the spread of household literature. Paradoxically, the ability to produce more books less expensively for a growing reading public encouraged publication of both more encyclopedic household manuals and more specialized ones. The range of the very popular *Inquire Within for Anything You Want to Know* is only barely indicated by four adjacent lines from its index: "Friends, Choice of them; Fritters, Batter for; From, or of?; Frost-bite, Treatment of." At the same time, works such as *Practical Vegetarian Cookery*, William Alcott's *Young Housekeeper*, C. A. Neal's *Total Abstinence Cookery*, and Lafcadio Hearn's *Cuisine créole* focus on very specific aspects of domestic life. New directions are indicated in *Trials and Confessions of an American Housekeeper*, which cloaks its advice in the accessible form of a housewife's musings (fig. 46). In addition, many works in this period—for example, Mary Virginia Terhune's *Eve's Daughters*, written under the pseudonym Marion Harland—combine domestic instruction with discussions of women's role in society. Nevertheless, volumes reflecting traditional attitudes about women and housework continued to find an audience, such as Alexander Murray's *Domestic Oracle*.

Winterthur's collection of nineteenth-century domestic treatises is especially impressive. Most influential writers on domestic economy are represented, including Sarah Josepha Hale, editor of *Godey's* from 1841 to 1877; Sarah Tyson Rorer, a cooking-school proprietor and author of *Home Games and Parties* as well as *How to Set the Table*; Mrs. D. A. Lincoln, another cooking-school proprietor who wrote *Mrs. Lincoln's Boston Cook Book*; and "American Orphan" Amelia Simmons, the first

Fig. 46. Title page, *Trials and Confessions of an American Housekeeper* (Philadelphia: Lippincott, Grambo, 1854). Page (trimmed): H. 6⁵⁄₁₆", W. 4³⁄₈".

Many nineteenth-century writers on domestic economy assumed an approach that was reassuring rather than dictatorial, couching their advice in fictional form in order to share common adversities of daily life—some of which are illustrated here.

CENTRE DISH — LE COQ GALLANT (A VOTRE SERVICE)

Fig. 47. "Centre Dish—Le Coq Gallant (a votre service)." From Theodore Francis Garrett, *The Encyclopaedia of Practical Cookery: A Complete Dictionary of All Pertaining to the Art of Cookery and Table Service*, vol. 7 (Philadelphia: Hudson Importing Co.; [London: A. Bradley], [1898?]), facing p. 512. Page: H. 11", W. 8⁵⁄₁₆".

Advances in the technology of color printing made possible this extravagant compendium of nineteenth-century cookery and table decoration.

native-born author of an American cookbook and seemingly the first to use cornmeal and cranberries in her cooking. The library collections also amply represent the gamut of cookbooks in the period from the insistently frugal to the extravagant. The dazzling color illustrations of Theodore Francis Garrett's *Encyclopaedia of Practical Cookery*, which features the creations of chef Francatelli, pupil of the great Carême and cook to Queen Victoria, demonstrate the heights to which Francatelli's influence could lead and belie the word *practical* in the volume's title (fig. 47).

As the century wore on, such major figures as Catharine Beecher, in her many publications, advocated greater system and order in the housewife's approach to her work, a demand that culminated in the "scientific household engineering" of the early twentieth century. Beecher, however, who believed the housewife a secular goddess and the inspiration of her household, might well have been confounded by the forthright sentiments of Christine Frederick, author of *Household Engineering*, who stated that before she discovered the scientific manner of handling household tasks, their repetitive drudgery made her long for the world of work she had given up for housewifery.

Whatever the century and whoever the author, cookbooks, receipt books, and manuals of domestic economy are primary tools for understanding the routines and objects of everyday life, especially their intended appearance, use, and care, as well as the value that their owners placed on them. They also record changes in daily life brought about by urbanization and technological innovation and the corresponding change in the housewife's role and view of her role. Above all, because they concern those ordinary matters that engage us still, they appeal directly to today's readers.

The Shakers

Fig. 48. William F. Winter, Shaker furniture, ca. 1936. Photograph; H. 9½″, w. 7½″.

This photograph first appeared as plate 16 in Edward Deming and Faith Andrews's *Shaker Furniture: The Craftsmanship of an American Communal Sect*. By the time the Andrewses' book came out in 1937, Winter had been photographing Shakers and their goods for nearly a decade. Winter's early death in 1939 at the age of forty robbed modern observers of additional insightful pictorial representations of the Shakers. The kind of round table pictured here was commonly built for sisters' and brothers' retiring rooms, while the four-slat rocker made in 1801 forecasts a style of Shaker furniture known to us today. Shaker men routinely used wooden spit boxes of the type seen here, which were filled with either sawdust or shavings.

Unlike many religious sects that appear only to vanish quickly or become part of the mainstream, the United Society of Believers in Christ's Second Appearing (the Shakers' official title) has successfully separated itself from the rest of the world since its beginnings in the mid eighteenth century. During this time, the sect's membership has numbered anywhere from a handful to thousands and has included men and women from all walks of life, mechanics and intellectuals alike. While the living movement is nearing an end, the history of the Shakers will remain with us forever, in part because of their artifacts. In addition to providing succeeding generations with a reminder of the Shakers, these artifacts offer historians a legacy that religious offshoots seldom bestow: a coherent expression of their spiritual values through material culture. In calling one of his books *Religion in Wood*, noted Shaker scholar Edward Deming Andrews recognized the relation of artifact to spiritual life in Shaker communities. As theologian Thomas Merton wrote in the introduction to Andrews's book, "The peculiar grace of a Shaker chair is due to the fact that it was made by someone capable of believing that an angel might come and sit on it. Indeed the Shakers believed their furniture was designed by angels." Fortunately, Andrews preserved images of Shaker furniture and other artifacts in his books through the photography of William F. Winter, whose work stands out for its welcome understanding of Shaker crafts (fig. 48).

Winterthur Library is extremely fortunate in having the extensive Shaker collection gathered by Andrews and his wife, Faith, who first became acquainted with the Shakers in 1923 at Hancock, Massachusetts. In their memoirs, *Fruits of the Shaker Tree of Life*, they recorded their first and subsequent encounters with the Shakers. During the course of time, the couple earned the trust and respect of the Shakers and were given countless gifts of Shaker imprints, manuscripts, photographs, and what we now call ephemera. After serving as primary resources for their many books, articles, and lectures, these materials were donated to Winterthur Library and formally dedicated in 1969 as the Edward Deming Andrews Memorial Shaker Collection. In 1987, a guide to its contents was published.

The materials in the Andrews Collection mirror the rise, progress,

Fig. 49. *Second Family, Mount Lebanon, New York*, ca. 1865–75. Stereograph; H. 3¾", W. 7".

The Shaker village in this view deserves the accolades bestowed on Shaker communities by Robert Wickliff in a speech before the Kentucky state senate in 1881: "In architecture and neatness they [the Shakers] are exceeded by no people upon the earth. Their villages and towns bear testimony everywhere of their skill in the mechanic and manufacturing arts. The whole society live in unexampled neatness, if not elegance—not a pauper among them—all alike independent. . . . Who has visited one of the Shaker villages, that has not experienced emotions of delight at the peacefull, harmonious, but industrious movements of the villagers" (quoted in *The Shakers: Life and Production of a Community in the Pioneering Days of America, an Exhibition by the "Neue Sammlung," Munich* [Munich: Staatliches Museum für angewandte Kunst, 1974], p. 65).

and decline of the Shaker movement from the late eighteenth to the late twentieth century. To become a Shaker, a prospective member had to sign a covenant in which he or she vowed to observe the tenets of the sect. The first covenant came from the New Lebanon (formerly Mount Lebanon), New York, community in 1795 and was revised through the next century to reflect changes in Shaker doctrine. Quite possibly persons considering membership in the society in the 1790s learned something about it from the first Shaker publication, Joseph Meacham's *Concise Statement of the Principles of the Only True Church According to the Gospel*, pulled from the Bennington, Vermont, press of Haswell and Russell in 1790.

Once in the society, members often recorded their routines and special concerns in manuscript diaries and letters. While some diaries in the Andrews Collection lack attribution, many name their keepers on a front leaf. The entries of Benjamin Gates, a New Lebanon resident, reveal the multitude of tasks that a typical Shaker brother was expected to perform, while the 1805 diary of Benjamin Seth Youngs relates an extraordinary trip that he and two others took to try to establish the society in the West. Relations among Shaker communities, especially in the West, are brought to life in more than 100 letters that comment on the uncertainties of wilderness existence and the perceived unsupportiveness of the home ministry at New Lebanon.

Other materials in the Andrews Collection concern the early forceful leader of the Shakers, Ann Lee. When Mother Ann died in 1784, nearly every Shaker immediately thereafter relied on the memories of Lee's contemporaries for details about her teachings. As more time passed, it became increasingly difficult to maintain the order without its charismatic leader or these personal memories. Lee's teachings and counsel were passed on, however, through spirit messages, which are communications the spirit of Lee sent to followers who then committed them to paper. Such messages in Winterthur Library are Rufus Bishop's "Words of a Shining Roll Sent from Holy Mother Wisdom to Brother Rufus Bishop, July 10th, 1842," and Mary Hazard's sketch of hearts on pages 191 and 192 of her hymnbook.

In addition to documenting the Shakers through the written word and drawings, the Andrews Collection offers researchers opportunities to study the Shakers through approximately 1,400 illustrated items, including prints, watercolors, postcards, stereo views, daguerreotypes, labels, and photographs. A stereo view of a Shaker village in New Lebanon testifies to the orderliness of Shaker life (fig. 49), while a seed advertisement from the same community bespeaks the Shakers' horticultural success (fig. 50). A photograph of members of the New Lebanon community preparing to dine suggests something of the social relations of the group (fig. 51). No doubt, Anthony Imbert's delicately colored lithograph depicting the "square order shuffle," a Shaker dance, is the most famous image in the Andrews Collection. However, Joshua Bussell's watercolor views of Shaker villages are the most original as they reflect the work of mid nineteenth-century folk artists so well (pl. 12). The library's collection of photographs, which show at least fifteen Shaker communities, for the most part spans a fifty-year period beginning around 1880. Interspersed

Fig. 50. *Shakers' Genuine Vegetable & Flower Seeds, from Mount Lebanon, Columbia County, N.Y.,* [ca. 1800s]. Advertisement; H. 11¼", W. 23".

According to an account book, Shakers at the New Lebanon community first systematically grew seeds to sell in 1795. At first, sales were limited to the local area, but as time passed, the "Shaker seed wagon" found receptive buyers in all parts of the country as well as in Europe.

Fig. 51. *North Family, Mount Lebanon, New York*, ca. 1890. Photograph; H. 4¾″, W. 7¾″.

The Shakers were well known for their excellent food. Because of the sect's reliance on hard work in its fields and manufactories, members had to be provided with substantial amounts of nourishing food. In this photograph, the sisters of the North Family at the New Lebanon community are preparing the long tables for a meal.

among photographs of individual communities are several series of pictures that show what the Shakers looked like and how they lived. A set of 32 stereographs entitled *Photographic Views, Shaker Village, Canterbury, New Hampshire*, by W. G. C. Kimball of nearby Concord, is representative of such assemblages.

Historians and observers of the Shaker movement started writing in the eighteenth century and have not stopped yet. Among the best known non-Shaker works are *New America* by William Hepworth Dixon, *Les Shakers Américains* by Henri Desroche, *American Communities* by William Alfred Hinds, *Three Villages* by William Dean Howells, and *History of American Socialisms* by John Humphrey Noyes. The most prolific writer that the Shakers can claim for themselves is Frederick William Evans whose works are represented by 83 imprints in the Andrews Collection. His *Tests of Divine Inspiration, Shakers: Compendium of the Origin, History, Principles, Rules, and Regulations*, and autobiography all contain a wealth of information about Shaker religious thought and practices. Not every author wrote in glowing terms about the Shakers, however. Three individuals who at one time resided with them, Thomas Brown, Eunice Hawley Chapman, and Valentine Rathbun, published exceedingly hostile accounts about their sojourns with the society.

One reason why some researchers study the Shakers is that the Shakers' detachment from worldly concerns makes them easy to understand as a group, while their varied activities and talents provide a number of ways to inquire into their collective life-style. The material in the Edward Deming Andrews Memorial Shaker Collection reflects the paradox of the Shakers' homogeneity and diversity.

Advertising

Printed and manuscript advertisements have existed ever since craftsmen realized that it was advantageous to promote themselves and their merchandise. In the world of eighteenth-century craftsmen, for example, a furniture maker might paste a rudimentary label or chalk his initials inside a piece to show the public the kind of work that might be expected from him. By recording his name on a product, the craftsman enhanced his reputation, indicated to retailers what he could supply, and at least implied to buyers that he would stand behind his work. Broadening the range of their promotions a bit further, craftsmen began placing advertisements in newspapers or city directories, noting their addresses and detailing their products, sometimes with illustrations. In addition to containing such simple advertisements, Winterthur Library houses colorful manuscript catalogues, printed trade catalogues, trade cards and labels, and billheads with illustrations and descriptions of products.

Among the most informative types of advertising literature to researchers is the trade catalogue. Strictly defined, trade catalogues are printed books, pamphlets, or broadsides issued by a maker so retailers could order merchandise for their stores' shelves. In practice, however, "trade catalogue" has come to mean just about any piece of promotional literature that describes a product. Benjamin Franklin is acknowledged to have issued the first printed American trade catalogues in 1744.

An outstanding manuscript catalogue that has survived into the twentieth century is a multivolume work compiled by an unnamed vendor in early nineteenth-century France (pl. 13). A splendid pictorial encyclopedia of middle-class products of the Napoleonic era, this catalogue's nearly 1,600 watercolors show a broad range of household products, personal goods, and miscellanea such as Argand lamps, gloves, tobacco boxes, scent bottles, dog collars, pistols, and toys. Even though these volumes originated in continental Europe, their contents were undoubtedly exported to and marketed in the United States. In fact, Lewis Page, a toy dealer from New York, is known to have ordered items from Europe just like the ones presented in this anonymous French catalogue.

Although the French catalogue is the library's most splendid, it is far from being its earliest. Dated 1760, the earliest American catalogue in the

Fig. 52. Teapot. From Benjamin Hadley, [*Catalogue*] (Birmingham, Eng., [ca. 1815]), no. 944. Page: H. 10¼", W. 17".

Hadley's catalogue includes plated ware and glass goods such as candlesticks, bottles, pitchers, trays, teapots, coffee urns, and sugar baskets. Even though this catalogue depicts English goods, such items were routinely available in the United States through an active network of trade. Handwritten notes in French on some leaves suggest that Hadley also had business interests in France. While the quality of the contents and condition of the plates make this catalogue important in trade literature, it is also significant because the manufacturer whose wares it illustrates can be identified. Very few late seventeenth- and early eighteenth-century catalogues can be linked to specific makers.

collection is from James Rivington, a Loyalist printer and bookseller who had just opened his shop in New York. The contents of its sixty-four pages indicate that a wide variety of books lately imported by Rivington was available. Other eighteenth-century catalogues at Winterthur, chiefly from England, represent a wide range of products, including hardware, silver articles, tableware, and tools. Unfortunately, the great majority of them lack attribution. Chief among the exceptions are the catalogues from the brass foundries of John Barker and Jee, Eginton, and Company; the silversmithing firms of Love, Silverside, Darby, and Company and Younge, Greaves, and Hoyland; toolmakers John Wycke and William and Samuel Butcher; and lampmaker John Miles. The products of these and other foreign craftsmen were regularly shipped to America.

During the late nineteenth and early twentieth centuries, trade catalogues grew in importance as American commerce expanded and printers began using chromolithography and photography. These developments spurred an explosion of catalogues for all kinds of products, from agricultural implements to food, from plumbing equipment to personal provisions. The library's collection, which is described in *Trade Catalogues at Winterthur*, emphasizes products associated with the home and items used by the people who lived in these homes. Glassware, ceramics, art supplies, wallpaper, silverware, paint, stoves, clothing, and statuary are all represented by trade catalogues in the collection. But by far the largest group of trade catalogues in the library comes from furniture makers. Some furniture catalogues are from manufacturers, such as the Leo Austrian company in Chicago, which made a variety of furniture forms, while

Fig. 53. Geo. Howe and Company, trade card, Lynn, Mass., ca. 1877. Card: H. 3½", W. 5¾".

This trade card was initially circulated by Spencer Optical Manufacturing Company of New York, a firm that claimed to be the "makers of the largest variety of spectacles & eye glasses in the world." The name of a local retail outlet, in this case Geo. Howe and Company, was then added to the front of the card. Manufacturers commonly provided retailers with cards that could be altered to include the names and addresses of local retailers.

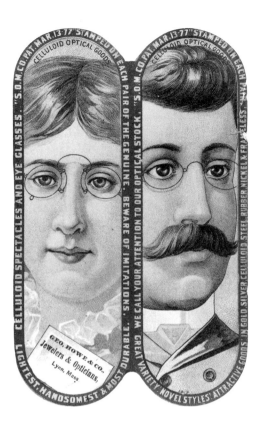

others, such as Buffalo Upholstering, Walter Heywood Chair, and Wooton Desk Manufacturing companies specialized.

Trade cards are yet another important resource for researchers. One of the thousands of trade cards at Winterthur is that of Benjamin Hadley of Birmingham, England, who made and sold silver-plated ware and glass products during the early decades of the nineteenth century. His trade card is pasted inside the front cover of his catalogue, which contains more than 150 plates illustrating the products he furnished to his customers (fig. 52). Most of the library's trade cards and labels, however, date from the second half of the nineteenth century and are part of the Thelma Seeds Mendsen Collection. In addition to those in the Mendsen Collection, the library has a representative selection of nineteenth-century trade cards. These include cards from Geo. Howe and Company, a jewelry and optical firm in Lynn, Massachusetts (fig. 53); Chas. Counselman and Company, a meat-packing concern in Chicago (fig. 54); and Willcox and Gibbs Sewing Machine Company in New York (fig. 55). Each depicts to twentieth-century observers one aspect of life a century and more ago and suggests different strategies of advertising: appeals through clever design, humor, and sentiment.

Fig. 54. Chas. Counselman and Company, Royal Ham trade cards, Chicago, ca. 1875–90. Cards (each): 4¾″ by 2⅞″.

This firm of meat packers relied on levity to relay its message to customers. Contributing to the company's humorous campaign are trade cards depicting a pig on a throne, another driving a cart to market, Indians, the Alabama Traveler, and two smartly dressed gentlemen.

Fig. 55. Willcox and Gibbs Sewing Machine Company, trade card, New York, 1876. Card: H. 3¼″, W. 9″.

This trade card, which was used at the Centennial Exhibition in Philadelphia in 1876, contrasts the domestic distress created in the household by an inferior sewing machine (*top*) and the domestic tranquility of the household that has a Willcox and Gibbs machine.

Several earlier trade cards, however, deserve special mention. One attractively printed trade card from 1800 concerns the activities of Trott and Bumstead, Boston merchants who operated an importing business. Their card announced that they had acquired and were selling "cheap, all kinds of European & India goods [and] looking glasses, in great variety." A 1771 billhead—a cousin of the trade card—engraved by Paul Revere reveals that Joshua Brackett, another Bostonian, charged a customer at Cromwell's Head for liquor and lodging his horse. A trade label for Philadelphian Samuel Taylor, a book binder and stationer, indicates that during the 1770s, Taylor bound "all sorts of Books, in the Neatest Manner, Gilt or Plain, as now Practised in England &c." And in 1701, Thomas Tuttell of London told the public through a set of now very rare playing cards that he sold mathematical and measuring instruments.

The library's collection of advertising literature augments the knowledge researchers gain in examining art and artifacts in the museum's unsurpassed collections. Indeed, the literature of advertising in its varied forms furnishes researchers with more pictures of documented artifacts than they might hope to see during years of visiting museums and historical societies.

Technology

The invention of printing during the fifteenth century had much to do with the development of technology. For the first time, information related to trades could be disseminated among the small literate segment of society. As literacy increased, the circle of knowledge grew correspondingly wider.

A survey of rare books in Winterthur Library reveals that early publications on technology were general histories covering many trades. Typical of such works is Thomas Powell's *Humane Industry; or, A History of Most Manual Arts*, which focuses on clocks and watches, artificial-motion machines, writing and printing, painting, spinning and weaving, glassmaking, and shipping and sailing. Coming at the end of the seventeenth century and portending the next century's trend toward works dealing with a single craft or process is Simon Barbe's *Parfumeur royal*, which contains a handsome frontispiece (fig. 56).

French, Dutch, and English technological publications of the eighteenth century range from treatises on individual trades and disciplines, such as Venterus Mandey's *Mellificium Mensionis; or, The Marrow of Measuring*, to dictionaries, encyclopedias, and instructional manuals on a host of experiments and procedures. The most famous is Denis Diderot's *Encyclopédie*, cherished for both its stunning essays and its exquisite engravings (fig. 57). An equally impressive but less well known series is *Descriptions des arts et métiers*, which appeared from the early 1760s through the late 1780s. Winterthur Library has acquired a nearly complete set of this important work.

In the wake of the eighteenth century, science and technology formed a comfortable, symbiotic alliance, with each feeding the other. No doubt the success of this alliance was fostered by the interest of both the gentry and the middle classes in improved technology. Although eighteenth-century gentlemen disdained actual physical labor, they had no aversion to experimenting and tinkering with the help of such aids as the *Gentleman's Companion; or, Tradesman's Delight* or J. Leadbeater's *Gentleman and Tradesman's Complete Assistant; or, The Whole Art of Measuring and Estimating, Made Easy*. Meanwhile, middle-class tradesmen and manufacturers increasingly consulted works such as *Nouveau dictionnaire*

Fig. 56. "Lorigine des parfums." From [Simon] Barbe, *Le parfumeur royal; ou, L'art de parfumer* (Paris: Chez Augustin Simon Brunet, 1699), frontispiece. Page: H. 6½″, w. 3¼″.

In this seventeenth-century illustration, raw materials for perfume making are extracted from plants and animals, while the ship on the horizon symbolizes trade with faraway shores.

universel des arts et des sciences and *Valuable Secrets Concerning Arts and Trade*. The interest in science and technology shared by these two groups is evident in such consumer products as the fine carriages pictured in *The Nobleman and Gentleman's Director and Assistant in the True Choice of Their Wheel-Carriages* (fig. 58).

While gentlemen, merchants, and manufacturers found both general and specific works on the crafts useful, governments during the eighteenth century also began to embrace technology. William Lewis's *Commercium Philosophico-Technicum*, for example, contains an acknowledgment to the king in which Lewis asserts that "the advancement of arts, trades, and manufactures, and the extension of commerce" are the "immediate objects" of the king's concern since they embody the "most certain means of

Fig. 57. "Agriculture, Labourage." From Denis Diderot, *Recueil de planches, sur les sciences, les arts libéraux, et les arts méchaniques, avec leur explication . . .*, vol. 1 (Paris: Briasson, David, Le Breton, Durand, 1762), pl. [1]. Page: H. 15½″, W. 9½″.

This engraving from Diderot reminds us that technology in early modern Europe often began on the land. The small letters and numbers superimposed on the engraving refer to detailed descriptions of tools used in eighteenth-century agriculture and husbandry.

attaining your darling wishes, the rendering Your people powerful and happy, and perpetuating the blessings of peace" (p. [i]). Nowhere is governmental interest in technology more apparent, however, than in canal technology. A rapidly growing means of attaining commercial blessings, canals were the focus of Robert Fulton's 1796 *Treatise on the Improvement of Canal Navigation*, which provided exquisitely detailed illustrations and guidelines for canal construction and design.

During the nineteenth century, new types of technological publications arose. Manufacturer's catalogues, such as that of Crompton Loom Works of Worcester, Massachusetts, began appearing, often with stunning illustrations. Fittingly, the Crompton catalogue uses technologically advanced chromolithography to advertise its sophisticated machinery (fig. 59). Despite such innovations, older forms of technological writing continued to be popular. Many American and foreign technological works of the nineteenth century focused on single trades or combined short textual descriptions of an array of trades with beautiful engravings. Sometimes such books were published for the benefit of children, both to educate them and perhaps to assist them in eventually choosing a craft vocation. Certainly among the handsomest of these works is a Dutch publication entitled *Geheel Nieuw Groot en Vermakelizk Prentenboek voor Kinderen*, in which each description of a trade is accompanied by a marvelous color illustration (pl. 14).

In the early stages of their country's development, Americans measuring their technological sophistication sometimes compared themselves unfavorably with Europeans. Expressing some hesitancy about the accomplishments of Americans in the preface to *One Thousand Valuable Secrets in the Elegant and Useful Arts*, a Philadelphia author in 1795 wrote: "Although the useful and necessary arts and manufactures, which

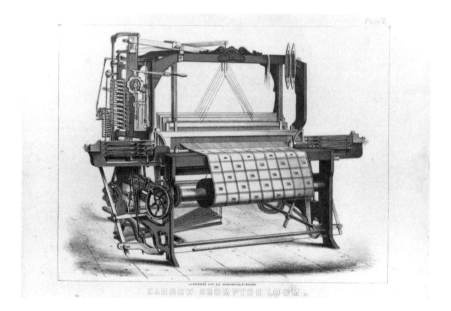

Fig. 59. "Narrow Crompton Loom."
From Crompton Loom Works, *Illustrated Catalogue of Looms, and Parts of the Same* (Worcester, Mass., 1868), pl. 5. Page: H. 11″, W. 8″.

This color illustration of a Crompton loom handsomely documents the coming of industrialization to the textile industry.

have mostly hitherto employed the industrious citizens of America, have acquired a degree of perfection, which rivals the production of Europe, those, which are distinguished by elegance and refinement are but little known, or at best in their infancy" (p. [iii]). Attempting to remedy the situation, the author included in his thousand secrets tips on engraving, varnishing, glassmaking, gilding, dying, mold crafting, inkmaking, winemaking, confectionery making, spot and stain removal, and fishing.

Improvements in American technology were promoted both by individuals and by organizations devoted to this purpose. In its 1817 address, Connecticut Society for the Encouragement of American Manufactures linked commerce, manufacturing, and agriculture as "the three great columns that support the dome of American prosperity" (p. 21). No longer the stepchild of science and philosophy, technology was increasingly applied to daily life. The words *practical* and *useful* appear constantly in the titles of nineteenth-century technological works. Technology was also promoted by the educational system, as is demonstrated by Marshall Perry's 1832 textbook, *First Book of Fine and Useful Arts for the Use of Schools and Lyceums*. After the Civil War, technology aided in improving health in the home. Carl Pfeiffer in his *Sanitary Relations to Health Principles in Architecture* reminded readers that good heating, ventilation, and lighting were essential in the home since "the dwelling exercises a more decided influence upon our health than the clothes we wear" (p. [3]).

Thus, having begun as the somewhat mysterious preserve of the relatively few, technology by the late nineteenth century had entered the privacy of the home, giving it a dynamism and practicality it never before had.

Travel

Travel narratives from the eighteenth and nineteenth centuries contain illuminating descriptions of the world before the camera and ever-improving transportation systems made touring ordinary and somewhat predictable. Americans today can easily travel to Europe or our national parks by airplane or automobile. Consequently, modern travelers tend to write about their experiences less often and in less detail than their counterparts of a century and more ago. The details that travelers in the past dutifully recorded in letters, diaries, and sketchbooks provide invaluable glimpses of past cultures to modern historians. Responses to spectacular events and natural wonders as well as observations about such routine matters as weather, dress, and accommodations indicate how earlier Americans viewed themselves and people from other lands.

In addition to narratives of their journeys, some artist-travelers produced extraordinary visual works depicting their travels. An unidentified traveler from Boston created eighty-one watercolors and pencil sketches in his travels up and down the Atlantic seaboard from Canada to Cuba (fig. 60), while Edwin Whitefield recorded informative text and sketched

Fig. 60. *Belvidere.* From Boston artist, manuscript diaries, vol. 2 (1857–64), pl. 2. Watercolor; H. 6½″, W. 9¾″.

Although the written observations of the artist who painted this scene are informative, the sketches he made during his travels between 1851 and 1864 offer a vision of nineteenth-century buildings and life-styles that might otherwise be lost. Pictured here is the Charleston, South Carolina, home of the Brewster family.

the American countryside in his diary. Among the most striking volumes in the library, no doubt, is John Collins's *Views of the City of Burlington, New Jersey*. Remaining in the vicinity of his adopted Philadelphia, Collins sketched and painted views of the historically notable buildings of that town (pl. 15).

Of the many forms of literature created by travel writers, manuscript travel accounts are among the most consistently reliable and refreshing. The library's earliest manuscript narrative of an excursion in the United States was written by an unnamed Philadelphian—probably a member of the Richardson family—who traveled from his hometown to Boston with a friend in 1791. The library's earliest narrative of an American's trip to a foreign land was written in 1796 and 1797 by Benjamin Johnson, a successful printer and Philadelphia Quaker, who was headed to France to try to mend a rift in the Society of Friends at Congenies. Johnson's account is atypical compared with others in the library since Johnson makes cerebral comments about the appearance of European cities, their inhabitants, and living conditions instead of merely describing the sights tourists normally went to see.

Manuscript travel narratives were often inspired by their author's need to ensure his own or his firm's commercial success. Success for the Philadelphia printing firm Kimber and Richardson necessitated that a member of the company spend part of 1813 traveling through Pennsylvania and Virginia plying books and magazines. As indicated by the "Sea Journal," the hope for success in another part of the world kept a supercargo busy at sea and in the Orient in 1804. Apart from recording the conditions and occurrences of oceanic sailing, the supercargo's manuscript details trading conditions that Westerners had to contend with in Calcutta and Canton. Remarks about the hong merchants of Canton are particularly valuable in unraveling the complexities of East–West relations two centuries ago, while the recitation of the relative value of currencies provides an index for comparing the riches of numerous countries. Of equal historical interest is the description of the unenviable situation of foreign traders in Manila. Informative travel accounts were also kept by seamen aboard merchant and military vessels. Francis Nichols's journal of his four-month voyage in 1812/13 aboard United States frigate *Chesapeake* records numerous encounters with enemy British ships. The *Chesapeake*, which was subsequently captained by James Lawrence, was taken by the British only three months after Nichols's voyage ended, losing a battle to the *Shannon* thirty miles off Boston harbor.

Some Americans in earlier ages traveled to satisfy their curiosity about natural wonders and foreign cultures. Naturalist John G. Bell was fortunate in combining his scientific and commercial interests on a

MEMPHIS . TENESSEE.   DIE STADT MEMPHIS . TENESSEE.

Fig. 61. "Memphis. Tennessee." From Henry Lewis, *Das illustrirte Mississippi-thal* . . . (Dusseldorf: Arnz, [1857]), facing p. 354. Page: H. 8″, W. 11″.

Like many painters of American scenery born in Europe, Henry Lewis was a native of Great Britain. He came to the United States with his father and brothers when he was ten years old. From 1846 to 1848, Lewis sketched while traveling up and down the Mississippi in order to prepare himself for the panorama he planned to paint showing the river in all its glory. After exhibiting his panorama in America, Lewis returned to Europe, married, and settled in Dusseldorf, Germany, where he published a volume of Mississippi scenes.

Panamanian hunting expedition in 1849/50. Bell's faithfully kept diary indicates that he found many species on which to practice his profession of taxidermy. Not until the mid nineteenth century did grand tours of Europe become fashionable in some quarters. While the names of their keepers have not survived the years, two of the library's manuscript diaries contain detailed travel narratives written by young men sightseeing in western Europe in 1852 and 1853. Their remarkable recall of architectural, historical, and topographical minutiae, however, suggests that they may have spent more time reading and then copying from their guidebooks than actually sightseeing. More informative about the experiences and attitudes of Americans touring Europe is the journal of Mary Patton, the wife of well-known nineteenth-century Presbyterian and Congregational clergyman William Patton, written during her combined grand tour and wedding trip in 1860/61. Another fascinating account of such tours is provided by Estelle M. Mendinhall, a society matron of Wilmington, Delaware, who traveled through both Europe and Egypt in 1905/6.

Just as Americans traveled to view European treasures, many Europeans left their native lands to see for themselves the country that had enticed their former countrymen to relocate and begin their lives anew in America. Artists, never to be left behind, numbered among them. Karl Bodmer (pl. 16), Henry Lewis (fig. 61), John Hill (fig. 62), Joshua Shaw, and Edward Beyer all gave nineteenth-century armchair travelers an opportunity to visualize America without having to leave home.

Fig. 62. John Hill, "Passaic Falls, New Jersey." From Joshua Shaw, *Picturesque Views of American Scenery* (Philadelphia: M. Carey and Son, [ca. 1820]), n.p. Page: H. 14½", W. 21".

Both John Hill, the engraver of this plate, and Joshua Shaw, the author of the work in which it appears, immigrated to America after winning artistic recognition in their native England. This plate illustrates how Paterson, New Jersey, appeared before industrialization forever altered it in the late nineteenth century. According to Shaw, the Passaic River flowed through Paterson "with a gentle and almost imperceptible current over beds of limestone, through rich and graceful scenery, till within a short distance of a deep cleft in a rock which crosses the bed of the river" (facing pl.).

While European travel appealed to Americans of means during the eighteenth and nineteenth centuries, excursions through the United States attracted other Americans. In 1839, for instance, Mrs. James Bogert records that her family from New York City crossed their state to visit Niagara Falls, while the anonymous "Remeniscences of Our Trip to the Columbian Exposition" documents the ten-day excursion of a Buffalo family. David Clapp, a printer, took his first trip by water from Boston to New York in 1831 and wrote about it with youthful enthusiasm. Writing of a similar journey some ten years later, Clapp, now a seasoned traveler, makes matter-of-fact comments, his exuberance apparently abated by familiarity and repetition.

Just as reports of explorations played a significant part in early American settlement, so did printed books circulated in European countries to encourage immigration to America. Two by William Penn are of special historical significance: *Some Account of the Province of Pennsilvania in*

America, printed in London in 1681, and *A Letter from William Penn, Proprietary Governour of Pennsylvania in America*, which contains a description of the province of Pennsylvania and a map showing Philadelphia bounded by the Delaware and Schuylkill rivers.

As time passed and America's highway and railroad systems burgeoned, citizens were given more opportunities to travel. Consequently, more books and articles were published in an effort to describe and explain America to the general public, both here and abroad. Well-known writers, including Charles Dickens and James Fenimore Cooper, published works on their travels, as did relatively unknown observers William Bingley, William Faux, and Richard Parkinson.

Travel and exploration have been important elements of the American experience ever since the New World was sighted by Christopher Columbus, himself a member of an exclusive group of early global explorers. Historians can only be thankful that so many people who journeyed from their homes placed pen and brush to paper to record the events and spectacles of their trips.

Holdings Cited

Ackermann, Rudolph. *The Repository of Arts, Literature, Commerce, Manufactures, Fashions, and Politics.* Ser. 1, vols. 1–14; ser. 2, vols. 1–14; ser. 3, vols. 1–12. London: R. Ackermann, 1809–28. Library holdings: all vols. except ser. 3, vol. 12.

Adam, Robert, and James Adam. *The Works in Architecture of Robert and James Adam . . . .* 2 vols. London: By the authors, 1778, 1779.

Aitken, John, ed. *The Scots Musical Museum.* Philadelphia: By the editor, [1797].

Aladdin Company. *Aladdin Homes: "Built in a Day."* Bay City, Mich., 1919.

Alberti, Leon Battista. *The Architecture of Leon Battista Alberti in Ten Books . . . .* Trans. into Italian by Cosimo Bartoli and from Italian into English by James Leoni. London: Thomas Edlin, 1726.

———. *L'architettura di Leonbatista Alberti.* Trans. into Italian by Cosimo Bartoli. Florence: Appresso L. Torrentino, 1550.

Alcott, William Andrus. *The Young House-keeper; or, Thoughts on Food and Cookery.* Boston: G. W. Light, 1838.

Aldrich and McCormac. Illustrated price list. Troy, N.H., 188?.

Allair, C. D. *Paper Doll's Furniture: How to Make It.* New York: Anson D. F. Randolph, 1857.

Allen, John. *Victoria Regia; or, The Great Water Lily of America.* Boston: Dutton and Wentworth, 1854.

Allestree, Richard. *The Ladies' Calling . . . .* 2d impression. Oxford: At the theater, 1673.

Allgates, H. Gates Lloyd, Haverford, Pa. Photographs, ca. 1920.

Allison, Michael. Personal estate inventory. New York, April 17, 1855.

American Lady. *Lonely Hours: A Text-book of Knitting.* Philadelphia: E. Gaskill, 1849.

American Sunday-School Union. *City Sights for Country Eyes.* Philadelphia: By the union, 1856.

Andrews, Edward Deming. *Religion in Wood: A Book of Shaker Furniture.* Bloomington and London: Indiana University Press, 1966.

———, and Faith Andrews. *Fruits of the Shaker Tree of Life: Memoirs of Fifty Years of Collecting and Research.* Stockbridge, Mass.: Berkshire Traveller Press, 1975.

The Archer's Guide. London: T. Hunt, 1833.

Arnd, Daniel, and Peter Ranck. Account book, Lancaster Co. and Jonestown, Pa., 1791–1817.

Arrowsmith, H. W. and A. *The House Decorator and Painter's Guide.* London: Thomas Kelly, 1840.

Arrowsmith, James. *An Analysis of Drapery; or, The Upholsterer's Assistant.* London: Printed by M. Bell, 1819.

Aspinwall, W. H. *A Descriptive Catalogue of the Pictures in the Gallery of W. H. Aspinwall . . . No. 99 Tenth Street, New York.* [New York: Printed by W. C. Bryant, 185?].

Bachman, Mary Eliza. Annotations in *Album.* New York and Boston: David Felt, Stationer's Hall, n.d. Charleston, S.C., area, 1835.

Bailey, John. Illustrated billhead. New York, November 5, 1792.

Bakewell, Pears, and Company. Receipts. Pittsburgh, Pa., 1866, 1867, 1869.

Baldwin, Jabez. Account book. Salem, Mass., 1809–19.

Ball, Joseph. Pattern book. Longton, Staffordshire, Eng., ca. 1820–60.

Barbe, [Simon]. *Le parfumeur royal; ou, L'art de parfumer.* Paris: Chez Augustin Simon Brunet, 1699.

Barker, John. [*Catalogue of Furniture Hardware: Handles, Escutcheons, Hinges, Drawer Pulls, and Bells*]. Birmingham, Eng.: Barker, [ca. 1780].

Barlow, Francis. *A Booke Containing such Beasts as Are Most Usefull for such as Practice Drawing, Gravaeing, Armes Painting, Chaseing . . . .* London: Henry Overton, [ca. 1660].

Barnard, Sir John. *A Present for an Apprentice . . . with Rules for His Conduct to His Master, and in the World . . . .* London, 1642. Reprint. Philadelphia: J. Crukshank for James Williamson, 1774.

Barozzi, Giacomo [a.k.a. Giacomo da Vignola]. *Regola delli cinque ordini d'architettura di M. Iacomo Barozzio da Vignola.* [Rome, 1563?].

Belcher Mosaic Glass Company. Catalogue. New York, 1886.

Bell, John G. Diary. Panama, 1849/50.

Berain, Jean. *Ornemens inuentez par I: Berain*. Paris: Se Vendent Chez Thuret, [17??].

Berkshire Furnace. Account books. Berks Co., Pa., 1765–67, 1770–72, 1789–94.

Berquin, Arnaud. *The Blossoms of Morality: Intended for the Amusement and Instruction of Young Ladies and Gentlemen*. 2d American ed. Wilmington, Del.: Printed by Joseph Johnson, 1796.

Beyer, Edward. *Album of Virginia*. Richmond, 1858.

Biedler-Viken, Manhasset, N.Y. Photographs, John Hay Whitney house, Locust Valley, Long Island, N.Y., ca. 1943.

Bingley, William. *Travels in North America from Modern Writers with Remarks and Observations . . . .* London: Harvey and Darton, 1821.

Bishop, Rufus. "Words of a Shining Roll Sent from Holy Mother Wisdom to Brother Rufus Bishop, July 10th, 1842." New Lebanon, N.Y.

Blake, George E., pianoforte-maker. Advertising broadside. Philadelphia, 18??.

Blegny, Nicolas de. *Le bon usage du thé, du caffé et du chocolat pour la préservation et pour la guérison des maladies*. Lyon: Thomas Amaulry, 1687.

Bogert, Mrs. James. Diary of a western tour. New York to Niagara Falls, 1839.

Book of Prices of the United Society of Journeymen Cabinet Makers. Cincinnati, Ohio: By the society, 1836.

Boston artist. Manuscript diaries: excursions, fishing, and bird hunting. 2 vols. Atlantic seaboard, Canada to Cuba, 1851–54, 1857–64.

Boston Glass Manufactory. Billhead. Boston, 1824.

Boulle, André-Charles. *Nouveaux deisseins de meubles et ouvrages de bronze et de marqueterie*. Paris: Mariette, n.d.

Brackett, Joshua. Billhead. Boston, 1771.

Brathwaite, Richard. *The English Gentlewoman*. London: B. Alsop and T. Fawcet for Michaell Sparke, 1631.

British and Foreign School Society. *Manual of the System of Teaching Reading, Writing, Arithmetic, and Needle-work, in the Elementary Schools of the British and Foreign School Society*. London: Printed for the benefit of the society and sold by Longman, 1816.

Brookshaw, George. *Groups of Flowers, Drawn and Accurately Coloured after Nature with Full Directions for the Young Artist*. 2d ed. London: Thomas McLean, 1819.

Brown, Thomas. *An Account of the People Called Shakers: Their Faith, Doctrines, and Practice . . . to Which Is Affixed a History of Their Rise and Progress to the Present Day*. Troy, N.Y.: Parker and Bliss, 1812.

Brumbaugh, G. Edwin. Brumbaugh papers, 1912–83.

Brunetti, Gaetano. *Sixty Different Sorts of Ornaments*. London, 1736.

Buffalo Upholstering Company. *New Goods for 1884*. Buffalo, N.Y., 1884.

Butcher, William and Samuel. [*Catalogue*]. Sheffield, Eng., [ca. 1811].

Butler, Charles. *The American Gentleman*. Philadelphia: Hogan and Thompson, 1836.

——. *The American Lady*. Philadelphia: Hogan and Thompson, 1836.

Buttre, William. Trade card. New York, ca. 1813.

Calabrella, E. C. *The Ladies' Science of Etiquette and Handbook of the Toilet by Countess de Calabrella*. Philadelphia: T. B. Peterson, [186?].

Carroll, George D. *The Art of Dinner Giving and Usages of Polite Society*. New York: Dempsey and Carroll, 1880.

Carter, Charles. *The Complete Practical Cook; or, A New System of the Whole Art and Mystery of Cookery*. London: W. Meadows, 1730.

[Caswall, Edward]. *Sketches of Young Ladies and Young Gentlemen by Quiz*. New York: Wiley and Putnam and G. Dearborn, 1838.

[*Catalogue Containing Watercolor Drawings of Japanese Porcelain*]. 2 vols. N.p., [ca. 1850–99].

[*Catalogue of Doorknobs, Escutcheons, Door Knockers, Furniture Brasses, Sconces, Etc.*]. [Birmingham, Eng.?, ca. 1783–89].

[*Catalogue of Watercolor Drawings Depicting French Wares*]. Vols. 1, 4. France, [ca. 1810].

[*Catalogue of Furniture Hardware and Sconces*]. [Birmingham, Eng.?, ca. 1770].

[*Catalogue of Toys*]. Germany, 1818–39.

Catlin, George. *O-kee-pah: A Religious Ceremony and Other Customs of the Mandans*. Philadelphia: J. B. Lippincott [London printed], 1867.

Censor. *Don't; or, Directions for Avoiding Improprieties in Conduct and Common Errors of Speech*. New York: D. Appleton, 1891.

Chambers, William. *Designs of Chinese Buildings, Furniture, Dresses, Machines, and Utensils*. London: [John Harris], 1757.

Chapman, John Gadsby. *Chapman's American Drawing Book*. New York: J. S. Redfield, 1847.

Chapman, Eunice (Hawley). *An Account of the Conduct of the People Called Shakers in the Case of Eunice Chapman and Her Children since Her Husband Became Acquainted with That People and Joined Their Society.* Albany, N.Y.: Printed for the author, 1817.

Chas. Counselman and Company. Royal Ham trade cards. Chicago, ca. 1875–90.

Chesterfield, Lord. *Principles of Politeness, and of Knowing the World, . . . with Additions by the Rev. Dr. John Trusler . . . .* Philadelphia: Mathew Carey, 1800.

Chippendale, Thomas. *The Gentleman and Cabinet-Maker's Director.* London: By the author, 1754.

Chippendale's Ornaments and Interior Decorations in the Old French Style Consisting of Hall Glass and Picture Frames, Chimney-pieces, Stands for China . . . . London: John Weale, [183?].

Church, Frederic Edwin. Letters. Colombia and Ecuador, 1853.

Cipriani, Giovanni Battista, and Francesco Bartolozzi. *Cipriani's Rudiments of Drawing Engraved by F. Bartolozzi.* London: G. Bartolozzi, 1786.

Clapp, David. Travel journals. Eastern seaboard states, 1831, 1841, 1843.

Clinton, Louisa. Watercolors, interiors of Scottish country homes, 1830s.

Coiffures. Twelve watercolor drawings; three heads in ovals, France, 1780–89.

A Collection of Figures and Conversations, Cattle, Birds, Beasts, and Landskips Neatly Engraved on Seventy-two Copper Plates: From Vernet, Boucher, Bergham, Barlow, Etc. London: Robert Sayer, 1771.

Collins, John. *Views of the City of Burlington, New Jersey, . . . Taken from Original Sketches.* Burlington, 1847.

Comenius, Johann Amos. *Orbis Sensualium Pictus.* London: Printed by J. R. for Abel Swall, 1689; London: Printed for S. Leacroft, 1777.

A Compleat Book of Ornaments Consisting of a Variety of Compartments, Shields, Masks, Prizework, Moreskwork, &c., Being Very Useful for Painters, Carvers, Watch-makers, Gravers, &c., Invented and Drawn by Some of the Best Artists. London: Thomas Bowles, [174?].

Connecticut Society for the Encouragement of American Manufactures. *Address.* Middletown, Conn.: Printed by T. Dunning, 1817.

Cooley, E. *A Description of the Etiquette at Washington City . . . during the Session of Congress.* Philadelphia: L. B. Clarke, 1829.

Cooper, James Fenimore. *Notions of the Americans Picked up by a Travelling Bachelor.* Philadelphia: Carey and Hart, 1833.

Cox, David. *A Treatise on Landscape Painting and Effect in Water Colours.* London: S. and J. Fuller, 1814.

———. *The Young Artist's Companion.* London: S. and J. Fuller, 1825.

Crapo, Henry H. Watercolors, William J. Rotch house, New Bedford, Mass., ca. 1880.

Crofton, John Saville. *The London Upholsterer's Companion, Containing the Most Approved and Modern Methods for the Various Styles of Manufacturing, Including the Art of Spring Stuffing . . . .* London: John Williams, 1834.

Crompton Loom Works. *Illustrated Catalogue of Looms, and Parts of the Same.* Worcester, Mass., 1868.

Crunden, John. *The Joyner and Cabinetmaker's Darling.* London: A. Webley, 1770.

Cuvilliés, François de. "Morceaux de caprice à divers usages." In *Oeuvres deuxième serie.* Munich: Se Vend Chez L'auteur, 1745.

The Dairy and the Poultry Yard. [London]: Joseph Myers, 1850–99.

Davis, Alexander Jackson. Correspondence, drawings, and photographs, William J. Rotch house, New Bedford, Mass., 1848–1867.

Deblois, Lewis. Trade card. Boston, 1757.

Descriptions des arts et métiers. Paris: Académie des Sciences, 1761–88.

Desroche, Henri Charles. *Les Shakers Américains: D'un néo-christianisme à un presocialisme.* Paris: Editions de Minuit, 1955.

[Dewing, Maria Richards (Oakey)]. *Beauty in the Household.* New York: Harper and Brothers, 1882.

Diary of an American on tour. 1853.

Diary of a young American in Europe. 1852/53.

Dickens, Charles. *American Notes for General Circulation.* London: Chapman and Hall, 1842.

Diderot, Denis. *Recueil de planches, sur les sciences, les arts libéraux, et les arts méchaniques, avec leur explication . . . .* 8 vols. Paris: Briasson, David, Le Breton, Durand, 1762– 72. Supplement to *Encyclopédie; ou, Dictionnaire raisonné des sciences, des arts, et des métiers, par une société de gens de lettres.* 28 vols. Paris: Briasson, 1751–72.

Dixon, William Hepworth. *New America.* Philadelphia: J. B. Lippincott, 1867.

Dominy, Felix. Account book. East Hampton, N.Y., 1818–27.

Dominy, Nathaniel, IV, and Nathaniel Dominy V. Account book B. East Hampton, N.Y., 1762–1844.

Dominy, Nathaniel, V. Account book and daybook. East Hampton, N.Y., 1798–1847.

Ducerceau, Paul Androuet. *Ornement servant aux brodeur ouvrier en soie et orfevre et autre.* Paris, [ca. 1660–1710].

Dummer, George. Account book. Jersey City Glass Works, Jersey City, N.J., 1847–48.

Eastman, Seth. *Treatise on Topographical Drawing.* New York: Wiley and Putnam, 1837.

The Edward Deming Andrews Memorial Shaker Collection. Comp. E. Richard McKinstry. New York and London: Garland Publishing, 1987.

Edwards, George, and Matthias Darly. *A New Book of Chinese Designs.* London: By the authors, 1754.

Endicott, George. Inventory. New York, 1848.

Evans, Frederick William. *Autobiography of a Shaker and Revelation of the Apocalypse.* Albany, N.Y.: Charles Van Benthuysen and Sons, 1869.

——. *Shakers: Compendium of the Origin, History, Principles, Rules and Regulations, Government, and Doctrines of the United Society of Believers in Christ's Second Appearing . . . .* New York: D. Appleton, 1859.

——. *Tests of Divine Inspiration; or, The Rudimental Principles by Which True and False Revelation, in All Eras of the World, Can Be Unerringly Discriminated.* New Lebanon, N.Y.: Shakers, 1853.

Fanny Gray. Boston: Crosby, Nichols, 1854.

Faux, William. *Memorable Days in America: Being a Journal of a Tour to the United States Principally Undertaken to Ascertain by Positive Evidence the Condition and Probable Prospects of British Emigrants . . . .* London: W. Simpkin and R. Marshall, 1823.

Fellow, R. *The Game of Croquet.* New York: Hurd and Houghton; Boston: E. P. Dutton, 1865.

Fenton, Christopher. Daybook. Bennington, Vt., 1847–59.

Fletcher, Thomas. Letter book. Philadelphia, 1852–59.

Forepaugh, Adam. *Catalogue of Living Wonders: Rare Animals and Birds to Be Seen at Adam Forepaugh's Great Zoological and Ornithological Menagerie and Museum . . . .* Buffalo, N.Y.: Printed by Warren, Johnson, 1871.

Formal Garden, Winterthur. Autochromes, 1910–16.

The Forty Thieves: A Drama. London: Benjamin Pollock, 1850–58.

Fowler, Orson Squire. *A House for All; or, A New, Cheap, Convenient, and Superior Mode of Building.* New York: Fowlers and Wells, 1848.

Fréart de Chambray, Roland. *A Parallel of the Antient Architecture with the Modern, in a Collection of Ten Principal Authors Who Have Written upon the Five Orders.* Trans. John Evelyn. London: Printed by Theodor Roycroft for John Place, 1664.

Frederick, Christine (McGaffey). *Household Engineering: Scientific Management in the Home, . . . a Correspondence Course on the Application of the Principles of Efficiency Engineering and Scientific Management to the Every Day Tasks of Housekeeping.* Chicago: American School of Home Economics, 1923.

Frezier, Amedée François. *Traité des jeux d'artifice.* Paris: Nyon, 1747.

Frickinger, Johann Michael. *Nützliches in lauter auserlesenen, wohl-approbirt- und meistentheils Neu-inventirten Mustern bestehendes, Weber-Bild-Buch . . . .* Neustadt and Leipzig: Jacob Samuel Friedrich Riedel, 1783.

Fulper Brothers. Pictorial price list. Flemington, N.J., 188?.

Fulton, Robert. *A Treatise on the Improvement of Canal Navigation; Exhibiting the Numerous Advantages to Be Derived from Small Canals.* London: I. and J. Taylor, 1796.

Galli da Bibiena, Ferdinando. *Direzioni a' Giovani Studenti nel disegno dell'architettura civile . . . .* 2 vols. Bologna: Nella Stamperia de Lelio dalla Volpe, 1777–83.

Galloway Terra-Cotta Company. *Galloway Pottery for Garden and Interior.* Philadelphia, [ca. 1905].

[*Gardiners Island Glass Catalogue*]. 2 vols. Gardiners Island, N.Y., [ca. 1805]. Owned by Johannes Schiefner of Bohemia.

Garrett, Theodore Francis. *The Encyclopaedia of Practical Cookery: A Complete Dictionary of All Pertaining to the Art of Cookery and Table Service.* 8 vols. Philadelphia: Hudson Importing Co.; [London: A. Bradley], [1898?].

Gates, Benjamin. "A Day Book or Journal of Work and Various Things Kept by Benjamin Gates, beginning October 1st 1827." New Lebanon, N.Y., 1827/28.

Gauger, Nicolas. *Fires Improv'd; Being a New Method of Building Chimneys, so as to Prevent Their Smoking . . . .* London: F. Senex and E. Curll, 1715.

——. *La mécanique du feu . . . .* Paris: Jacques Estienne and Jean Jombert, 1713.

Geheel Nieuw Groot en Vermakelizk Prentenboek voor Kinderen. Zalt-Bommel, Netherlands: Johannes Noman, 1826.

The Gentleman's Companion; or, Tradesman's Delight. London: Printed for J. Stone, 1735.

Geo. Howe and Company. Trade card. Lynn, Mass., ca. 1877.

Gilbert, Ann Taylor. *City Scenes; or, A Peep into London.* London: Harvey and Darton, 1828.

Gilpin, Thomas. Inventory. Philadelphia, 1839–41.

[Gourdoux-Doux, J. H.] *Elements and Principles of the Art of Dancing, as Used in Polite and Fashionable Circles.* Philadelphia: J. F. Hurtel, 1817.

[Gracian y Morales, Baltazar]. *The Courtiers Manual Oracle; or, The Art of Prudence*. London: M. Flesher for A. Swalle, 1685.

Graff, Frederick. Drawings in pen, pencil, and watercolor, Philadelphia, 1798–1806.

Gregory, John. *A Father's Legacy to His Daughters*. Chambersburg, Pa.: Dover and Harper for Mathew Carey, 1796.

Griffiths and Browett. [*Catalogue*]. Birmingham, Eng., [ca. 1860].

Grohmann, Johann Gottfried. *Recueil d'idées nouvelles pour la décoration des jardins et parcs*. Paris: Fuchs, 1796.

Guillim, John. *A Display of Heraldry*. London: Printed by S. Roycroft for R. Blome, 1724.

Guilmard, Désiré. *Le garde-meuble, ancien et moderne*. Paris: D. Guilmard and Bordeaux, [18??].

Hadley, Benjamin. [*Catalogue*]. Birmingham, Eng., [ca. 1815].

Hale, Sarah Josepha, ed. *Godey's Magazine*. New York: Godey Co. Vols. 14–95 (January 1837–December 1877). Library holdings (title and editors vary): Vols. 1–137 (July 1830 – August 1898).

[Hall, Florence Marion (Howe)]. *The Correct Thing in Good Society*. Boston: Estes and Lauriat, 1888.

Handloom weaver. Draft design book. Probably France, nineteenth century.

Harris, Kate S., comp. Textile sample books. Salem Co., N.J., 1882.

Hassell, John. *Aqua Pictura*. 2d ed. London: Hassell, 1818.

Haven, Alice Bradley. *"All's Not Gold That Glitters"; or, The Young Californian*. New York: D. Appleton, 1865.

Hazard, Mary. "A Collection of Songs of Various Kinds Written and Pricked for the Purpose of Retaining Them, by Mary Hazard; beginning June 16th, 1839." New Lebanon, N.Y.

Hearn, Lafcadio. *La cuisine créole . . . .* 2d ed. New Orleans: F. F. Hansell and Brother, [1885].

Henshaw, auctioneer. *A Catalogue of the Neat and Elegant Household Furniture, Prints, Books, etc. Belonging to Sir George Cheywynd, Bart., of Brocton Hall . . . which Will Be Sold at Auction . . . , 1803*. Stafford, 1802.

Hill, John. Aquatint engravings for *The Hudson River Port Folio*. New York: Henry T. Megarey, [1828].

Hinds, William Alfred. *American Communities: Brief Sketches of Economy, Zoar, Bethel, Aurora, Amana, Icaria, the Shakers, Oneida, Wallingford, and the Brotherhood of the New Life*. Oneida, N.Y.: Office of the American Socialist, 1878.

Hints to Men about Town; or, Waterfordiana . . . by a Sporting Surgeon. London: H. Smith, [ca. 1830].

The History of Little Fanny, Exemplified in a Series of Figures . . . . 2d ed. Philadelphia: Morgan and Yeager, 1825.

The History of Little Goody Twoshoes. Wilmington, Del.: Printed by Peter Brynberg, 1796.

Holt, Ardern. *Fancy Dresses Described; or, What to Wear at Fancy Balls*. London: Dekenham and Freebody, 1887.

Howells, William Dean. *Three Villages*. Boston: James R. Osgood, 1884.

Hullmandel, Charles Joseph. *The Art of Drawing on Stone*. London: Longman, Rees, 1835.

Huthwaite, Hannah. Cookery book. England, ca. 1712.

Ideas for Rustic Furniture. London: I. and J. Taylor, [178?].

Illustrated Pattern Book of English China and Earthenware; French China-ware, Plain and Ornamental; English and Foreign Flint Glass, Plain, Cut, and Engraved; Coloured and Decorated Glass; also of Chinese and Japanese China Ware, Parian and Terra-cotta Goods, Window and Plate Glass, Plain and Silvered, Mirrors, Looking Glasses, Mechanical Pieces, Flowers and Birds under Glass Shades, Pictures and Picture Frames, Stained Glass Windows and Panels; Table Ornaments, &c., Lamps, Globes, Chimneys, &c. N.p., [ca. 1880].

Imbert, Anthony. *Shakers near Lebanon, State of New-York*, [ca. 1830s]. Watercolor; H. 18½″, w. 22″.

Inquire Within for Anything You Want to Know . . . Particularly Intended as a Book for . . . All Subjects Connected with Domestic Economy . . . . New York: Garrett, Dick, and Fitzgerald, 1857.

Introduction to Drawing Ships. London: Robert Sayer, 1788.

J. G. and J. F. Low [Company]. *Illustrated Catalogue of Art Tiles*. Chelsea, Mass., 1884.

J. L. Mott Iron Works. *Illustrated Catalogue "Q" and Price List: Vanes, Bannerets, Finials, &c*. New York and Chicago, 1892.

James W. Tufts [Company]. *Descriptive Catalogue of James W. Tufts' Arctic Soda-water Apparatus*. Boston, 1876.

Jee, Eginton, and Company. [*Catalogue*]. Birmimgham, Eng., [ca. 1790].

Johnson, Benjamin. Travel diary in Europe. 1796/97.

Johnson, Madame. *Madame Johnson's Present; or, The Best Instructions for Young Women . . . with a Summary of the Late Marriage Act*. London: M. Cooper and C. Sympson, 1754.

Johnson, Thomas. *One Hundred and Fifty New Designs*. London: Robert Sayer, 1758.

Joseph Holmes Iron Works. Account books. Kingston, Mass., 1728–34, 1759–75.

Journal des Luxus und der Moden. Weimar. Vols. 1–42 (1786–1827). Library holdings: vols. 1–17 (1786–1802).

The Journeymen Cabinet and Chairmakers' New-York Book of Prices. New York: T. and J. Swords, 1796.

Kelley, Lilla Elizabeth. *Three Hundred Things a Bright Girl Can Do.* Boston: Page, 1903.

[Kenrick, William]. *The Whole Duty of a Woman by a Lady.* Exeter, N.H.: Stearns and Winslow, 1794.

Kilburn and Dodd. *A New Book of Sprigs of Flowers for the Use of Ladies, Tambour Workers, Etc.* London: Robert Sayer and J. Bennet, 1776.

Kimball, W. G. C. *Photographic Views, Shaker Village, Canterbury, New Hampshire.* Concord, N.H.: Kimball, [ca. 1880].

Kimber and Richardson. "[Journal of a Printer's Trip through Pennsylvania and West Virginia]." Philadelphia, 1813.

King, Nicholas. *A Plan, and Perspective View of a House and Other Buildings, Belonging to Mr. Edwd. Langley, on Square No. 651 in the City of Washington.* Washington, D.C., 1798.

Die Kleine Fanny. Leipzig: Karl Tauchnitz, [ca. 1815].

Knight, Frederick. *Knight's Gems or Device Book.* 2d ed. London: J. Williams, [183?].

———. *Knight's New Book of Seven Hundred and Fifty-eight Plain, Ornamented, and Reversed Cyphers.* Engraved by Nathaniel Gill and J. H. Whiteman. London, 1832.

———. *Knight's Scroll Ornaments, Designed for the Use of Silversmiths, Chasers, Die-sinkers, Modellers, &c., &c.* [London]: T. Griffiths, [1825–30].

———. *Knight's Unique Fancy Ornaments.* 5 parts, 4 [ornament designs] each or bound complete. London: J. Williams, 1834.

———. *Knight's Vases and Ornaments, Designed for the Use of Architects, Silversmiths, Jewellers, Modellers, Chasers, Die Sinkers, Founders, Carvers, and All Ornamental Manufacturers.* London: J. Williams, 1833.

Krimmel, John Lewis. Sketchbooks. 7 vols., 1810–21.

The Lady's Companion: Containing Upwards of Three Thousand Different Receipts in Every Kind of Cookery . . . Being Four Times the Quantity of Any Book of This Sort . . . . 2 vols. 5th ed. London: Printed for T. Read and R. Baldwin, 1751.

La Farge, John. Sketchbook. New York, 1862–64.

La Mésangère, Pierre de. *Collection des meubles et objets de goût . . . .* Paris: Pierre de La Mésangère, Au Bureau de Journal des Dames, [183?].

Laporte, John. *The Progress of a Water-coloured Drawing.* London: By the author, 1812.

Laurence, John. *The Clergy-Man's Recreation: Shewing the Pleasure and Profit of the Art of Gardening.* London: Printed for Bernard Lintott, 1717.

Leadbeater, J. *The Gentleman and Tradesman's Compleate Assistant; or, The Whole Art of Measuring and Estimating, Made Easy.* London: Printed for A. Webley, 1770.

Leaf and Flower Pictures and How to Make Them. New York: Anson D. F. Randolph, 1860.

Le Brun, Charles. *A Method to Learn to Design the Passions . . . .* Trans. John Williams. London: By the translator, 1734.

Le Nôtre, André. [*Garden Designs*]. Paris: N. Langlois, [168?].

Leo Austrian and Company. *Illustrated Catalogue.* Chicago, [ca. 1905].

Le Pautre, Jean. [*Ornament Suites*]. Paris: P. Mariette, [ca. 1660].

Lewis, Henry. *Das illustrirte Mississippithal, dargestellt in 80 nach der Natur aufgenommenen ansichten vom Wasserfalle zu St. Anthony an bis zum Golf von Mexico.* Dusseldorf: Arnz, [1857].

Lewis, William. *Commercium Philosophico-Technicum; or, The Philosophical Commerce of Arts: Designed as an Attempt to Improve Arts, Trades, and Manufactures.* London: Printed for H. Baldwin, 1763.

Library Committee of the R[ight] W[orshipful] Grand Lodge of Pennsylvania, Free and Accepted Masons. *Dedication Memorial of the New Masonic Temple, Philadelphia . . . .* Philadelphia: Claxton, Remsen, and Haffelfinger for the Library Committee, 1875.

Lincoln, D. A. [Mary Johnson Bailey Johnson]. *Mrs. Lincoln's Boston Cook Book: What to Do and What not to Do in Cooking.* 1883. Reprint. Boston: Roberts Brothers, 1888.

Lincoln, F. S. Photograph album, Bertha King Benkard house, Oyster Bay, Long Island, N.Y., 1945.

L'intérieur de la poupée. France, 1900–1909.

Little Helen; or, A Day in the Life of a Naughty Girl. New Haven: S. Babcock, 1825.

A Little Pretty Pocket-Book, Intended for the Instruction and Amusement of Little Master Tommy and Pretty Miss Polly. Worcester, Mass.: Isaiah Thomas, 1787.

Lock, Matthias. *Principles of Ornament; or, The Youth's Guide to Drawing of Foliage.* London: Robert Sayer, [174?].

Loir, Alexis. [*Suite of Ornament Etchings*]. Paris: N. Langlois, [ca. 1700].

Loudon, John C. *The Suburban Horticulturalist; or, An Attempt to Teach the Science and Practice of the Culture and Management of the Kitchen, Fruit, and Forcing Garden.* London: William Smith, 1842.

Love, Silverside, Darby, and Company. [*Catalogue*]. Sheffield, Eng., [ca. 1785].

Magazin für Freunde des guten Geschmacks. Leipzig: Friedrich August Leo, 1794–[1800]. Library holdings: nos. 1, 2 (1794); nos. 3, 4 (1795); vol. 1 (1795); vol. 2, nos. 1, 2, 3, 4, 5, 7 (1796); vol. 3, nos. 4, 5, 7, 8 (1797); vol. 4, nos. 1–8 (1798).

Magazzino di mobilia o sieno modelli di mobili di ogni genere. Florence: Società Calcografica, 1797–[98]. Library holdings: no. 1 (October 1796); no. 2 (March 1797).

Malton, James. *A Collection of Designs for Rural Retreats, as Villas, Principally in the Gothic and Castle Styles of Architecture . . . .* London: J. and T. Carpenter, [1802].

———. *An Essay on British Cottage Architecture . . . .* London: Hookham and Carpenter, 1798.

Mandey, Venterus. *Mellificium Mensionis; or, The Marrow of Measuring . . . .* London: Thomas Tebb, Sam Illidge, and Thomas King, 1727.

Map of the Valley of the Sacramento including the Gold Region. Boston: T. Wiley, Jr., 1848.

Marbury, Mary Orvis. *Favorite Flies and Their Histories.* Boston and New York: Houghton, Mifflin, 1896.

Marian Coffin Collection. Letters, drawings, and photographs, eastern seaboard of the United States, 1914–57.

Markham, Gervase. *Countrey Contentments, in Two Bookes . . . the Second Entitled the English Huswife . . . .* London: Printed by John Breale for R. Jackson, 1615.

Marks, Isabel. *Fancy Cycling for Amateurs.* London: Sands, 1901.

Marot, Daniel. *Werken.* Amsterdam, 1707.

Martick Iron Works. Inventory. Smithburg, Pa., 1768.

Maximilian Alexander Philipp, Prinz von Wied-Neuwied, *Reise in das Innere Nord-America in den Jahren 1832 bis 1834.* Coblenz: J. Hoelscher, 1839–41.

Maxine Waldron Collection of Children's and Paper Toys.

Meacham, Joseph. *A Concise Statement of the Principles of the Only True Church According to the Gospel . . . .* Bennington, Vt.: Haswell and Russell, 1790.

Meggendorfer, Lothar. *Das Puppenhaus.* Germany: By the author, [ca. 1895].

[Meissonier, Juste Aurèle]. *Oeuvre de Juste Aurèle Meissonier, peintre, sculpteur, architecte, et dessinateur de la chambre et cabinet du Roi.* Paris: Huquier, [ca. 1750].

Mendinhall, Estelle M. "Places Visited." 1905/6.

Mesker and Brother. *Architectural Catalogue [of Galvanized Iron Work].* St. Louis, Mo., 1888.

Miles, John. *Miles Patent Agitable Lamps.* Birmingham, Eng.: Miles, [ca. 1790].

Milton, Thomas. *The Chimney-piece-Maker's Daily Assistant.* London: H. Webley, 1766–69.

Milton Bradley Company. *Work and Play Annual.* Springfield, Mass., 1872.

The Mirror of the Graces; or, The English Lady's Costume . . . with Useful Advice on Female Accomplishments, Politeness, and Manners . . . by a Lady of Distinction. New York: I. Riley, 1813.

Mondon, Jean. *Neu Inventierte Vorstellungen von Stein und Muschel Werck mit Chinesischen Figuren verziert Dritter-Theil.* Augsburg: Johannes Georg Merz, [ca. 1750].

Morris, Richard. *Essays on Landscape Gardening and on Uniting Picturesque Effect with Rural Scenery: Containing Directions for Laying Out and Improving the Grounds Connected with a Country Residence.* London: Printed for J. Taylor, 1825.

Murray, Alexander. *The Domestic Oracle; or, A Complete System of Modern Cookery and Family Economy.* London: H. Fisher, Son, [1834].

A Museum and Panorama for Instruction and Amusement of Our Young Friends. Philadelphia: John Weik, [185?].

N. Clark and Company. Pictorial price list. Lyons, Mount Morris, and Rochester, N.Y., ca. 1835.

Neal, C. A. *Total Abstinence Cookery; Being a Collection of Receipts for Cooking, from which All Intoxicating Liquids Are Excluded.* Philadelphia: Eugene Cummiskey, 1841.

Nestell, Christian M. Drawing book. New York, 1811/12.

New Lebanon, N.Y., community. "Covenant of the Church of Christ in New Lebanon Relating to the Possession and Use of a Joint Interest," 1795.

Newton's New Game of Virtue Rewarded and Vice Punished for the Amusement of Youth of Both Sexes. London: William Darton, 1818.

Nichols, Francis. "A Journal of a Cruise on Board the United States Frigate *Chesapeake.*" 1812/13.

Nichols, Francis D. *A Guide to Politeness; or, A System of Directions for the Acquirement of Ease, Propriety, and Elegance of Manners, Together with a Variety of Approved Sets of Cotillons and Contradances.* Boston: Lincoln and Edmands, 1810.

Nivelon, F. *The Rudiments of Genteel Behavior.* [London?], 1737.

The Nobleman and Gentleman's Director and Assistant in the True Choice of Their Wheel-Carriages. London: Printed for A. Webley, 1763.

Northend, Mary Harrod. Glass-plate negatives, early New England decorative arts and architecture, ca. 1905–20.

Nouveau dictionnaire universal des arts et des sciences, français, latin et anglais. 2 vols. Avignon: François Girard, 1753.

Noyes, John Humphrey. *History of American Socialisms.* Philadelphia: J. B. Lippincott, 1870.

Old Hickory Chair Company. *Rustic Old Hickory Chairs, Rockers, Settees, Tables.* Martinsville, Ind., 1902.

One Thousand Valuable Secrets in the Elegant and Useful Arts, Collected from the Practice of the Best Artists. Philadelphia: Printed for B. Davis, 1795.

Orange County Flint Glass Works. Illustrated billhead. Port Jervis, N.Y., 1882.

Orr, Robert. Trade card. Philadelphia, 1796.

Ottaviani, Giovanni. *Loggie di Rafaele nel Vaticano*. Rome, 1772–77.

Page, Jeremiah. Account book. Danvers, Mass., 1761–62.

Page, Lewis. Letter book. New York, 1829–33.

Palladio, Andrea. *The Architecture of A. Palladio; in Four Books . . . to which Are Added Several Notes and Observations Made by Inigo Jones . . . .* Revised, designed, and published by Giacomo Leoni. London: John Watts, 1715–19.

Paper-doll costume. H. 12″. England, 1600–1649.

Papworth, John Buonarotti. *Hints on Ornamental Gardening: Consisting of a Series of Designs for Garden Buildings, Useful and Decorative Gates, Fences, Railroads, &c.* London: R. Ackermann, 1823.

Parkinson, Richard. *A Tour in America in 1798, 1799, and 1800 . . . .* London: Printed for J. Harding, 1805.

Passarini, Filippo. *Nouve inventioni d'ornamenti d'archittetura.* Rome: Domenico de Rossi, 1698.

Patton, Mary Shaw Bird. "Journal." 1860/61.

Peacham, Henry. *The Compleat Gentleman.* 1634. 3d impression. London: E. Tyler for R. Thrale, 1661.

Peale, Raphaelle, and Rembrandt Peale. Trade card. Philadelphia, 1793–96.

[Peddle, Mrs.] *Rudiments of Taste, in a Series of Letters, from a Mother to Her Daughters.* Chambersburg, Pa.: Dover and Harper for Mathew Carey, 1797.

Penn, William. *A Letter from William Penn, Proprietary and Governour of Pennsylvania in America, to the Committee of the Free Society of Traders of that Province Residing in London . . . .* London: Andrew Sowle, 1683.

———. *Some Account of the Province of Pennsilvania in America, Lately Granted under the Great Seal of England to William Penn . . . .* London: Benjamin Clark, 1681.

Perry, Marshall. *First Book of the Fine and Useful Arts for the Use of Schools and Lyceums.* Boston: Carter and Hendee, 1832.

Pfeiffer, Carl. *Sanitary Relations to Health Principles in Architecture.* New York: Francis and Loutrel, [1873].

Phébe; ou, La piété filiale. Paris: Didot le Jeune, 1817.

Philadelphia traveler. Diary of a trip from Philadelphia to Boston. 1791.

Phyfe, Duncan. Estate inventory. New York, 1854.

———. Invoices to Charles N. Bancker and George Newbold, New York, 1816.

———. *The New-York Revised Prices for Manufacturing Cabinet and Chair Work.* New York: Printed by Southwick and Pelsue [probably for the New-York Society of Journeymen Cabinet Makers], 1810.

———. Pencil drawings, chair designs, New York, ca. 1816.

[———]. *Peremptory and Extensive Auction Sale of Splendid and Valuable Furniture . . . at the Furniture Ware Rooms of Messrs. Duncan Phyfe and Son, Nos. 192 and 194 Fulton Street . . . New York.* New York: Halliday and Jenkins, 1847.

[Pichon, Thomas Jean]. *Sacre et couronnement de Louis XVI, roi de France et de Navarre, à Rheims, le 11 Juin 1775.* Paris: Chez Vente, Libraire des Menus Plaisirs du Roi, 1775.

Potts, Leslie. Watercolor renderings, room settings, Winterthur, 1948.

Powel, Samuel. Invoice book. Philadelphia, 1724/25.

Powell, Thomas. *Humane Industry; or, A History of the Most Manual Arts, Deducing the Original, Progress, and Improvement of Them.* London: Henry Herringman, 1661.

Pozzo, Andrea dal. *Rules and Examples of Perspective Proper for Painters and Architects . . . .* Trans. J. Sturt. London: J. Senex and R. Gosling; W. Innys; J. Osborn and T. Longman, [170?].

Practical House Carpenters' Society of the City and County of Philadelphia. *The Constitution of the Incorporated Practical House Carpenters' Society, . . . Together with Rules and Regulations for Measuring and Valuing House Carpenters' Work.* Philadelphia: By the society, 1812.

Practical Vegetarian Cookery. Ed. Countess Constance Wachtmeister and Kate Buffington Davis. San Francisco: Mercury Publishing; Chicago: Theosophical Book Concern, 1897.

The Protean Figure and Metamorphic Costumes. London: S. and J. Fuller, 1811.

La Psyché; ou, Le petit magasin de modes. France, 1820–29.

Ramapo Iron Works. Invoice. Haverstraw, N.Y., 1807.

Randolph, Anson Davies Fitz. *Paper Dolls and How to Make Them.* New York, 1856.

Randolph, Benjamin. Receipt book. Philadelphia, 1763–77.

Rathbun, Valentine. *Some Brief Hints of a Scheme Taught and Propagated by a Number of Europeans Living in a Place Called Nisqueunia in the State of New York.* New York, 1783.

"Remeniscenses of our Trip to the Columbian Exposition from August 21/93 to August 31/93."

Repton, Humphrey. *Fragments on the Theory and Practice of Landscape Gardening.* London: J. Taylor, 1816.

Richardson, Francis, Francis Richardson I, and Francis Richardson II. Account book. Philadelphia, 1684–1722.

Richardson, Joseph. Commonplace book. Philadelphia, 1744–52.

Richardson, Joseph, Jr. Letter book. Philadelphia, 1777–90.

——, and Nathaniel Richardson. Inventory. Philadelphia, May 31, 1790.

Riou, Stephen. *The Grecian Order of Architecture: Delineated and Explained from the Antiquities of Athens . . . .* London: J. Dixwell for the author, 1768.

Rivington, James. *A Catalogue of Books Lately Imported and Sold by James Rivington, Bookseller and Stationer from London.* New York: Rivington, 1760.

Robert Brost Stereocard Collection. 1935, 1938.

Robert Wemyss Symonds Collection. Photographs and documents, ca. 1920–58, English furniture, ca. 1450–1850.

Roberts, James. *The Sportsman's Pocket Companion.* [London: Henry Roberts, 1760?].

Robertson, Hannah. *The Young Ladies School of Arts; Containing a Great Variety of Practical Receipts . . . .* 4th ed. London, [1777].

Robinson, Peter Frederick. *Rural Architecture; or, A Series of Designs for Ornamental Cottages . . . .* London: Rodwell and Martin, 1823.

Rookwood Pottery. [*Catalogue*]. Cincinnati, Ohio, [ca. 1901].

The Room Beautiful. New York: Clifford and Lawton, 1915.

Rorer, Sarah Tyson [Heston]. *Good Cooking.* Philadelphia: Curtis Publishing; New York: Doubleday and McClure, 1898.

——. *How to Set the Table.* 19th ed. Haverhill, Mass.: H[orace] N. Noyes, [ca. 1910].

——. *How to Set the Table; Being an Treatise upon This Important Subject.* Wallingford, Conn.: R. Wallace and Sons Mfg. Co., 1910.

[Rowan, Archibald H.?] Sample book of designs for printed cottons, [Wilmington, Del., ca. 1795–96?].

Rutter, T. Drawing book, rustic furniture. London, ca. 1825.

St.-Sernin, Mlle. *Healthful Sports for Young Ladies.* London: R. Ackermann, [1822].

Scamozzi, Vincenzo. *L'idea della architettura universale . . . .* Venice, 1615.

"Sea Journal." Calcutta, Manila, Canton, 1804.

The Shakers: Life and Production of a Community in the Pioneering Days of America, an Exhibition by the "Neue Sammlung," Munich. Munich: Staatliches Museum fur angewandte Kunst, 1974.

Shaw, Joshua. *Picturesque Views of American Scenery.* Philadelphia: M. Carey and Son, [ca. 1820].

Sheraton, Thomas. *The Cabinet-Maker and Upholsterer's Drawing-Book.* London: Printed by T. Bensley, 1793–94.

Shillinglaw, Thomas E. B. *The Artists Complete Assistant in Drawing and Painting in Oil and Watercolours; with Instructions in Oriental and Mezzo-tinting; Crayon, and Velvet Painting; Tinted and Chalk Drawing; Transferring and Varnishing, &c.* Edinburgh, 1832.

[Simmons, Amelia]. *American Cookery; or, The Art of Dressing Viands, Fish, Poultry, and Vegetables; and the Best Mode of Making Puff-pastes, Pies, Tarts, Puddings, Custards, Pickles, and Preserves and All Kinds of Cakes, from the Imperial Plumb to Plain Cake, Adapted to this Country, and All Grades of Life.* New York: William Beastall, 1822.

Sloan, Samuel. *The Model Architect: A Series of Original Designs for Cottages, Villas, Suburban Residences, Etc. . . . .* 2 vols. Philadelphia: E. S. Jones, [1852].

——. *The Model Architect, Containing Original Designs for Cottages, Villas, Suburban Residences, Etc. . . . .* 12 parts. Philadelphia: E. S. Jones, 1851–52.

[Smith, E.] *The Compleat Housewife; or, Accomplish'd Gentlewoman's Companion . . . Collected from the 5th Ed.* Williamsburg: Printed by William Parks, 1742.

Smith, George. *A Collection of Designs for Household Furniture and Interior Decoration, in the Most Approved and Elegant Taste . . . .* London: J. Taylor, 1808.

Smith, John Rubens. *A Compendium of Picturesque Anatomy Applied to the Arts.* Boston: By the author, 1827.

Smitley residence, Schenectady, N.Y. Photographs, 1903.

Sonner, John H. Account ledger. Strasburg, Va., 1884–91.

Spode factory. Shape and pattern book. Stoke-on-Trent, Staffordshire, Eng., ca. 1815–21.

Stalker, John, and George Parker. *A Treatise on Japanning and Varnishing.* Oxford: John Stalker, 1688.

Stanley B. Ineson Collection.

Stickley, Gustave. Business records, Stickley and Simonds Co., Eastwood, N.Y., 1892–98; L. and J. G. Stickley, Fayetteville, N.Y., 1900–present; and Craftsman Workshops, Inc., Eastwood, N.Y., 1899–1916.

——. *Chips from the Craftsman Workshop.* New York: Gustav[e] Stickley, Craftsman, [1907?].

——. *Craftsman Homes.* New York: Craftsman Publishing Co., [ca. 1909].

——. Glass-plate negatives (and modern contact prints), furniture in Craftsman Workshops, Inc., Eastwood, N.Y., ca. 1905–16.

Stiegel, Henry William. Indenture. Manheim, Pa., 1774.

Stillé, Charles J. *Memorial of the Great Central Fair for the U.S. Sanitary Commission, Held at Philadelphia, June 1864.* Philadelphia: By the commission, 1864.

Sully, Thomas. Letters. London, 1837/38.

Swan, Abraham. *The British Architect; or, The Builders Treasury of Staircases . . . .* Philadelphia: R. Bell for John Norman, 1775.

Swank, [Samuel?]. Daybook. Near Johnstown, Pa., 1850–57.

Sympson, Samuel. *A New Book of Cyphers, More Compleat and Regular than Any Yet Extant.* London: By the author, 1726.

T. Knight and Son, London. *Suggestions for House Decoration.* London, 1880.

Taylor, Isaac. *Advice to the Teens.* 1st American ed. from the 2d London ed. Boston: Wells and Lilly, 1820.

Taylor, Samuel. Trade label. [Philadelphia, ca. 1775].

[Terhune, Mary Virginia (Hawes)]. *Eve's Daughters; or, Common Sense for Maid, Wife, and Mother, by Marion Harland [Pseud.].* New York: J. R. Anderson and H. S. Allen, 1882.

Terry, H., auctioneer. *A Catalogue of All the Neat Household Furniture . . . Plate, Linen, China . . . of Mr. John Gibbs, Farmer and Corn Dealer, which Will Be Sold . . . at His Late Dwelling House . . . 1803.*

Textile design album. [France, 1800–1849].

Thackery, Anna. Letter to Mary James, Warsash, Titchfield, Eng., September 23, 1867.

Thelma Seeds Mendsen Collection. Trade cards, greeting cards, calling cards, valentines, postal cards, etc., United States and Europe, ca. 1850–1925.

Thomas, Thomas. Drawings of a house by T. Thomas and Son, New York, 1840–49.

Topsell, Edward. *The History of Four-Footed Beasts and Serpents . . . Whereunto Is Now Added, the Theatre of Insects . . . by T. Muffet . . . .* London: Printed by E. C., 1658.

Townshend, Barbara Anne. *Introduction to the Art of Cutting Groups of Figures, Flowers, Birds, etc. in Black Paper.* London: Edward Orme, 1815–16.

Trade Catalogues at Winterthur: A Guide to the Literature of Merchandising, 1750 to 1980. E. Richard McKinstry. New York and London: Garland Publishing, 1984.

Tredgold, Thomas. *Practical Essay on the Strength of Cast Iron and Other Metals . . . .* 2d ed., impr. and enl. London: J. Taylor, 1824.

Trials and Confessions of an American Housekeeper. Philadelphia: Lippincott, Grambo, 1854.

Trimble's Iron Works. Correspondence. Kentucky, 1832.

Trott and Bumstead. Trade card. Boston, 1800.

Tuttell, Thomas. Playing cards. London, 1701.

Unteutsch, Friedrich. *Neues Zieratenbuch den schreinern Tischlern. . . .* Nuremberg: Paulüs Fürsten, 1635.

Valuable Secrets Concerning Arts and Trades; or, Approved Directions, from the Best Artists, for the Various Methods of Engraving on Brass, Copper, and Steel. Boston: J. Bumstead, 1798.

Vandewater, J. L., auctioneer. *Catalogue of the Household Furniture, to Be Sold . . . April 27, [186?].* New York, [186?].

Van Laar, G. *Magazijn van Tuin-Sieraaden.* Amsterdam: J. de Ruyter, [1802].

Van Schaack, Eliza T. *A Woman's Hand; or, Plain Instructions for Embellishing a Cottage, with Easy and Practical Lessons in Pellis or Leather Work, Oriental, Grecian Oil, and Italian Landscape Paintings.* Albany: Munsell and Rowland, 1859.

Various Sketches of Shipping, Designed as an Assistant for Youth towards Studying Marine Drawing. London: Robert Sayer, 1792.

Vecellio, Cesare. *Corono delle nobili et virtuose donne . . . .* Venice, [1600–1625].

Villa Gardener. 11 vols. London: Simpkin Marshall, 1870/71–1880/81. Library holdings: vols. 1, 2, 1870–72.

Vitruvius, Pollio. *I dieci libri dell'architettura di M. Vitruvio.* Trans. with commentary by Daniel Barbaro. Venice: Francesco Marcolini, 1556.

Vredeman de Vries, Jan. *Les cinq rangs de l'architecture . . . .* Amsterdam: Chez Jean Janson Marchand Libraire, 1617.

Walter Heywood Chair Company. *Rattan, Wood, Cane, and Upholstered Chairs.* New York, 1895.

Washington, George. "Account of the Furnishings of the Official Residences of the President in New York and Philadelphia." [Philadelphia], 1789–96.

[———]. Inventory of furnishings for the president's house. New York, 1789–96. 4 leaves.

"Waste Book." Philadelphia area, nineteenth century.

[Wells, Samuel R.] *How to Behave: A Pocket Manual of Republican Etiquette.* New York: Fowler and Wells, 1856.

Whitefield, Edwin. Diary. 8 vols. [Ca. 1855]–63.

Willcox and Gibbs Sewing Machine Company. Trade card. New York, 1876.

William Gomm and Sons. "Sundry Drawings of Cabinet Ware &c." London, 1755–63.

Winter, William F. "[Collection of Photographs]." New Lebanon, N.Y., and Hancock, Mass., among other locales, ca. 1936.

Winterthur Cottage. Photograph album, date unknown.

Wise, Daniel. *Minnie's Playroom; or, How to Practice Calisthenics.* Boston: George C. Rand, William J. Reynolds, 1854.

Withers and Buchanan. [*Catalogue*]. London, [ca. 1790].

Wood, John. *A Description of the Exchange of Bristol . . . .* Bath: Thomas Boddeley for James Leake, 1743.

Wooton Desk Manufacturing Company. *Catalogue of the Wooton Patent Cabinet Office Secretaries and Rotary Desks.* Indianapolis, 1883.

Wrightson, H. Sketchbook. England, 1817–20.

Wyke, John. [*Catalogue of Tools for Watch and Clockmakers*]. Liverpool and Prescot: Wyke, [ca. 1770].

Younge, Greaves, and Hoyland. [*Catalogue of Table, Bracket, and Chamber Candlesticks Manufactured in Silver or Plated Metal*]. Sheffield, Eng., [ca. 1790].

Youngs, Benjamin Seth. Diary. New Lebanon, N.Y., to the Midwest, 1805.

Notes on Contributors

WINTERTHUR LIBRARY

Katharine Martinez is Director, Library Division, and Librarian, Waldron Phoenix Belknap, Jr., Research Library of American Painting.

Bert R. Denker is Librarian in Charge, Visual Resources Collection.

Paul B. Hensley is Archivist, Winterthur Archives.

E. Richard McKinstry is Librarian in Charge, Joseph Downs Collection of Manuscripts and Printed Ephemera.

Neville Thompson is Librarian in Charge, Printed Book and Periodical Collection.

American Cornucopia
Treasures of the Winterthur Library

was typeset, printed, and bound in an edition of two thousand by
Meriden-Stinehour Press. The text type is Sabon, a typeface designed
by Jan Tschichold, and set on a Linotronic-300. The text paper is
Mohawk Superfine, and the endleaves are Rainbow Texture.
Two hundred handcrafted slipcases were made by
Judi Conant of Guildhall, Vermont.

Photography by Wayne B. Gibson.
Production and copy editing by Patricia A. Rice Lisk.
Editorial consulting by Jeanne M. Malloy.
Design by Christopher Kuntze.